Melissa Campbell graduated from Drake University Law School in 1998. She is a lawyer and mother and lives in Indiana with her daughter, Kaliana.

David Hildebrand graduated from Ball State University in 1990 and owns a fitness franchise. He is married to Cathy and has two daughters, Kailee and Rachel. David lives in Indiana.

Both Melissa and David have made healthy living a serious part of their lives and will continue to do so.

This book is dedicated to the gym teachers, the 80-year-olds lifting weights, the men watching the kids so their wives can focus on their fitness, and the middle-aged men hitting the gym at 5:00 am before work. To all of those who put in all the work and got none of the glory. You embody our message: You Matter. You are the real heroes.

Melissa Campbell and David
Hildebrand

YOU MATTER

Your Personal Health
Revolution

AUSTIN MACAULEY PUBLISHERS™

LONDON • CAMBRIDGE • NEW YORK • SHARJAH

Ordering Information:
Quantity sales: special discounts are available on quantity purchases by corporations, associations, and others. For details, contact the publisher at the address below.

Publisher's Cataloguing-in-Publication data
Campbell, Hildebrand, Melissa and David
You Matter

ISBN 9781645750628 (Paperback)
ISBN 9781645750635 (Hardback)
ISBN 9781645750642 (ePub e-book)

Library of Congress Control Number: 2020904746

www.austinmacauley.com/us

First Published (2020)
Austin Macauley Publishers LLC
40 Wall Street, 28th Floor
New York, NY 10005
USA

mail-usa@austinmacauley.com
+1 (646) 5125767

We would like to thank everyone who got up an hour early in the mornings to go work out—alone. Everyone who joined a gym despite others' warnings that they're too fat, too skinny, too old, too busy, etc. To those of you who shared a new personal record even though everyone was 'tired of hearing about it.' Who grocery shopped and meal prepped for good food items for their families even though they complained. For those who dedicated time each day to fitness and nutrition even though they were mocked. To everyone who dared to invest in themselves because YOU MATTER. You are the reason we do what we do.

Table of Contents

Introduction

We'd like to begin this book with a commentary from co-author, Melissa Campbell, regarding her experiences with living healthy. Her story is recognizable to each of us – either in the form of the person attempting to be healthy or the majority using slight cues to dissuade positive change. Please read this piece and understand that the attempt thereafter is to help you create a determined pathway toward success. Whose success? Yours!

Psychologists say that we are the average of the five people we spend the most time around. It is true that the people around us affect our personal success. This is more acute in areas of everyday life such as nutrition, health, and exercise. Our daily habits often coincide and are shaped by the habits of those we are closest to. Given the epidemic of sugar addiction, processed convenience foods, obesity, and the prevalence of a sedentary lifestyle, it's no wonder that in the area of health and fitness, this is more often a challenge than an asset. We take most of our meals with our families and our coworkers. It's those same people whom our daily routines most often brush up against.

From Melissa's experience with healthy living:

I have a dirty little secret that I generally keep to myself: I eat healthy. I nearly insist upon eight hours of sleep. I would cancel almost any plans to keep my daily appointment with myself to work out. I buy organic. I eschew chemicals. Amongst groups, I mainly keep this to myself. Once my secret is out, I take my place as the "health nut" and am lightly teased for my fastidious ways. But, it's really not that funny. Why am I explaining why I food prepped protein-rich organic Buddha bowls for my lunches for the week rather than my co-workers explaining to me why they eat drive-through fast food every day?

Recently, I filled out a form at my new office to sign up for my dish to bring to an upcoming pitch-in. I wrote in the blank: "A healthy vegetarian option that no one will really like." Yes, I did it to be funny. But why is it funny? I bring a dish so I know I can stick to my eating habits no matter the situation. And almost always, people ask for the recipe afterwards. So, maybe I can become one of someone's five and be a positive influence.

Living a healthy lifestyle, particularly if it reaps visible benefits of a healthy, lean appearance, will separate you from your peers, your coworkers, and your family. Success holds up a mirror to others. Every single time I mention the gym, I immediately hear, "I need to get back into a good workout routine." I don't mention it gratuitously or in a proselytizing manner. I may simply mention that I will "meet you for dinner after the gym," and arrive with still red cheeks from class. This will transform many interactions into either a critique of exercise programs or an endless lamenting of my companion's own health missteps – neither being what I had intended. Therefore, I often avoid letting out my "dirty little secret" of a dedication to fitness. I don't want to make people feel bad about themselves.

Recently, I said to a friend when she asked why I was so hot and sweaty, "I just returned from a run."

She said, "Hasn't it been determined that running is bad for us?" I did not want to have this conversation. I wasn't seeking praise (although I wouldn't mind it), but I certainly am not being irresponsible for taking a 3-mile run before our movie date. This is often another common response criticism. I hear how terrible weight lifting is for women, the potential for injury, the bulkiness, the fanatical diets...All the while, I've been lifting weights for 3 years, don't look bulky, and am fitter than ever at age 46. Why is it OK in our culture to deter fit-minded people?

The point is this: Living a healthy lifestyle is often alienating, isolating, and can create tension amongst those around you. This is an unfortunate fact.

Partners may feel threatened. Your success may point out their "failures." Your new enthusiasm for the gym or your new workout friends may make them uneasy. If you are losing weight, they may fear your appeal to others. There is a woman whose husband, upon her slimming down, began bringing home pizza and carry-out for dinner every night. He felt intimidated by her enhanced beauty. There is not an easy answer for this. Ideally, partners who love us will want what's best for us, but that is not often the case. Include your partner, encourage your partner, respect your partner, but I would urge you not to lose your resolve to become healthier and fitter. Have faith that by making good, healthy choices, you will make it through any initial tensions and get to a healthier, better place in life. You partner may either join you in becoming fit, become a part of your new circle of friends, or at the very least be supportive when he/she sees your improved health and happiness. Your partner will reap the benefits of your positive changes. Your will bring your happiness into the home. You will have the energy for your partner and family. Your confidence will likely improve your relationship by relieving minor stressors. Recognize that it is a common part of the journey, but it only a step. This tension may rear its ugly head at the beginning of your new lifestyle commitment. See it through. Have faith that your positive changes will influence those around you, and if that doesn't quite happen – at least others will become more at ease once their fears subside. Stay the course. You can think of your commitment to yourself, and also to your family in that you are modeling health and fitness and being your best for your family. That is something you can take pride in.

And from David's personal experience:

I was in Montana recently at the Billings Airport at a gift shop while waiting for my flight. I was wearing a T-shirt that I received for doing a bike ride in Indiana called RAIN. It was a 160-mile bicycle ride that was accomplished in one day. The lady at the checkout asked me if I did this ride and when I said "yes," she said confidently, "Wow – you must be in really good shape." I said "yes," thanked her and went to my flight. Later in the flight, I realized a fundamental issue with her comment that I think pervades society. Why not say "Wow – you must be healthy." Maybe being healthy is implied by the "good shape" comment but

I think it goes deeper than that. Seemingly dismissed from our culture is the connection that being fit and in good shape also leads to a healthy person. As though, the reason that I'm in good shape is to complete a bicycle ride when it's backwards. I completed the bicycle ride as a statement of my good health and needed to be in good shape to do this. Isn't there a connection between being healthy and being in good shape too?

Welcome to this book! We have a goal to simplify your approach to healthy living by clarifying what you already know but choose not to do. We want to show you that being healthy is not a function of gimmicks nor extreme sacrifice but good, honest healthy eating, effective exercise, and proper sleep. Following some basic advice is all that is needed for your improvements to be dramatic and durable.

We've structured the book to not be chronological so that you can go to sections most applicable to you. We are strong believers in making improvements as quickly as possible and want you to be in charge. You should pick your chapters to read based on your interest and where you will get the biggest return on your reading time.

The format of the book starts where it should start. And that is with you. This is your life that you are working on. This is an unapologetic self-help book. You are the reason for the book and by even picking it up and reading this far, you know that you are wanting direction on a lifestyle for you and your loved ones that skips the BS and is quickly usable. Our goal is to provide this to you in the following pages. The flow of the book is to address why being healthy and fit begins with your emotional state. The "why" of self-improvement is seldom addressed and just presumed. As Melissa stated earlier, you'll practically get accosted for living a healthy lifestyle and, therefore, you need a usable mindset to provide answers to these forthcoming charges. This is why we address your emotional state first. Without it, you'll struggle.

The step following the "why" of a healthy lifestyle is the "how." Now that we've gotten the "why" better understood, our hope is that the normal self-improvement mechanisms make valuable sense to you and are easier to implement. Exercise, nutrition, and rest make up the obvious part of this information. Also, we know that many will have children and/or loved ones that you include in your inner circle. I've tried to address them as well to give you food for thought on how to address their needs too. The topic of children is included in each chapter. Apply this information to whomever it fits. Open your circle up to include anyone you honestly touch.

Does this self-improvement stuff cost? Yes and no. We've included an Economics chapter to give you a usable philosophy showing that this investment pays off handsomely.

Acknowledging that a lot of information out there is confusing is important as well, we've included a chapter called Myths and Untruths to give you cause to question the validity of information coming at you.

We do have one exception to the randomness of the book and that is regarding the confidant section. Read this and begin your journey here. The point of this is that you may need some time to discover this person, and we want you to know as soon as possible what to look for. The benefits of the confidant make the struggle to find this person worth it. Your health and fitness cannot wait. We have all watched the effects of the buy this/buy that approach along with the go-it-alone choice or the "internet search approach," none of which is working. Trying to do any of these things harder or smarter will not change the result.

A trusted confidant will see that you accomplish your goals. We want you to start here first so that you can consider your path to this person. When found, you will find your journey easier, more successful, and durable. All wins for you!

Chapter One
Confidant

I spend a lot of time in this book discussing the value of confidants and encourage you to find one that you trust to guide you forward to a truly healthier you and an honestly better life. Not a frilly, fancy person – just a no-nonsense source of information whose honest interest is your betterment.

Have you ever had a coach for YOUR life? Someone in your corner to help keep you on track and manage your health, wellness, nutrition, and fitness? What does this person look like, and how can you tell if you have the right one?

Great questions and now for some answers. I have no interest in making this hard.

This person (your confidant) is a seeker of knowledge. Loves science and is skeptical of marketing. New products are very slow to impress them and only after true data is available will they look in a new direction. I am a believer that the majority of the book you are about to read contains little to no new information. You already know most of this stuff, you just don't do it. Having said that, this person is a strategic planner on your behalf, motivates you, and holds you accountable. Genuine interest in you is a must-have criterion. Easy is best, and common sense towards living will transcend new and sexy. Gadgetry will play a small to no role in their approach. Time tables and measurable will, though.

This person will truly want you to succeed and will follow you wherever you are to insure you are on track. This is a package find (healthy minded, actively does healthy themselves, cares about others, and has room for you!) This is going to be hard so you will need to allow for a few misses to narrow you in. Do not lose time. Use this book to cover the gap. Get going! Do not wait on the perfect setup. Get to living healthy right now! Eat right, exercise right, sleep right, get your stress under control, etc. All of these will help you discover your chosen confidant.

Do you need a confidant? Yep – we all do. All the way from those who struggle with a single sit-up or push-up, find yourself out of air at the slightest task, overweight and unhealthy, to those who are struggling to find a lifestyle that YOU want. Professional athletes already have them. The better college teams have them on staff. I'm here to tell you that YOU MATTER and are important. Get one of these people in your corner so you can have a complete and fulfilled life. You matter!

So – what should you do? Your task is to get to work and find this person and engage them. You're to develop a relationship with this person that transcends money and that you can speak to regarding any subject without worry of judgment. Topics will come up that are seemingly easy to solve for acquaintances but you know require a deeper logic. This confidant is who you use and you know they will take *all* variables into consideration prior to suggesting a solution. Have this kind of bond. Where do you look to find this gem? What do the early steps look like? Great questions, and the probable answers include fitness fanatics who have little regard for their own success. They're a little past their prime but still honestly engaged in their own health. These folks are ready to pass the torch and share what they've learned. A lot of trials have occurred in their path and they're done with the nonsense and mirror worshipping. You might have someone like this in your life now. Your approach to them is a no BS, can-you-help-me conversation. The expectation for you is to already have had your own internal conversation to determine if you are sincere. Because when you approach this person, be ready for action. They'll be more excited than you and ready to help. Let them. The challenges they will lay in front of you are real – get to work and get rid of the "I can't" BS. They will not want to hear it. Don't be afraid to ask why. If the answer makes great sense to you, you are just confirming your choice as right. As I mentioned earlier, not a lot of new knowledge will come from this book – eat right, exercise right, sleep right, and get your stress under control.

You are on your way.

What are other positive attributes to a great confidant? A stranger who is moderately or not connected to you is a good attribute as they will accept less of your baggage. They will worry about you – not your BS. This person doesn't watch the clock to see when they can get out of the situation – their sincere interest is a positive solution for everyone involved. Strangers are treated the same as friends. This person is somewhat politically un-savvy – they will tell you what you need to be told and not necessarily be nice about it.

What are the early steps in finding a solid confidant? The first thing you do is – get to work. Your time is important and the sooner you start, the more honest you will be with yourself and the more careful you will be in accepting a confidant into your life. Now that you're to work, keep your eye out for an honestly trustworthy candidate. This can be a personal trainer as they tend to live the talk or if you feel that you have someone in your sights, begin by observing them. Are they behaving with sincerity?

Begin your dialogue with them and be honest. This is a big choice and a lot rides on being right. Hopefully, you already know who the right person is but maybe haven't approached them yet. If you think that you know, you should be a little sly regarding this discovery. Observances of people will guide you most accurately to your chosen confidant. The best early steps include observing from a distance and seeing how the person cares and acts towards normal and abnormal situations. Does this person intercede to make things better with little regard to their own gain? If yes, this is a good sign. If not, move on. This is important – find the right person and create a two-way communication platform. The need to be honest with each other is crucial to your success!

Does this cost money? Probably – you need to be OK with that. Accept this reality. The most expensive things you have were "free." Cheap or "free" advice that is bad costs a lot of money and lost time. I've heard the excuses that others around you are more important, and I'm not here to argue with you on this point. I am here to give you a nudge to raise your own bar and understand that the healthier you are, the more involved you can be with those around you. They appreciate the new you and you enjoy events more! View this as an investment and not a purchase. Investments and purchases are not the same thing, as investments pay you back with interest. Good investments cost nothing! Your money back plus. Keep in mind the value of lower healthcare costs, lower food bills, generally willing and able to say "yes" to opportunities. You should understand that too many good things do not happen due to excuses. Up your bar, enjoy your life, and save money too! Win! Win! Win!

Another valid way to look at this opportunity is to understand that you are never going to be younger than you are right this second. I'm personally encouraging you to make your life a priority right now. If you wait five years to begin, you are five years older and usually in worse shape than you are right now. Do not wait!

"The greater danger for most of us lies not in setting our aim too high and falling short; but in setting our aim too low, and achieving our mark."

—Michelangelo

Get a great confidant and "set your aim higher." You might still miss but with help, hitting a high target will happen and be worth it!

Welcome to the book. Let's make this thing happen!

Chapter Two
Myths and Untruths

Myths and untruths are very powerful in the world of health and fitness. Each year, powerful marketing machines craft new messages and update old ones designed to remove you from your money and in return you will get a trinket promising major positive changes in your life for next to no effort!!! Wow! – what BS.

This is a major pet peeve of mine as everyone wants to do the right thing for themselves and their loved ones and they should be congratulated and have good, accurate information available to them so they can honestly choose the right path.

Instead, they are beguiled into believing that all forms of self-improvement are to be vanity based and have just minor differences between them and the choice should just come down to price. This problem is so bad that I've seen advice from money managers telling people to ditch their gym memberships to save money. What??? If you want to save money, get healthy and do not get sick. This is what gyms really should do.

My advice is to be a critical thinker regarding the information out there. Using the usual axiom: if it sounds too good to be true, it probably is. Truer words couldn't be spoken. Be selfish on these points. Answer this: What is your goal? What will make this honestly happen? And then go from there. A big point is to make sure that you go deep in the goal making process. Assign some time for a heart-to-heart with your confidant and require yourself to not leave the discussion without a sincere goal and a plan to achieve it.

So, what's out there that readily confuses people and causes them to behave in a way that prevents success?

Let's start with some of the myths that screw people up:

MYTH: A Calorie Is a Calorie

You know, a calorie from a soda is the same as a calorie from a lentil. While it's true that both have calories, the difference to your body is startling. The calories from the soda are foreign to your body and it basically doesn't know what to do with them. The result – your body gives up and throws insulin at the sugary mix and sends the stuff to fat. Hence, these are considered empty calories. Diet soda may not contain any calories itself but causes cravings to make you eat more than you normally would have. (Plus the outlandish damage to your bones.)

Another issue that I have with soda is that as people give them up, they tend to get headaches. To me, any item that causes me to get a headache if I choose to quit that item, has been engineered to addict me to the item, and this is completely unacceptable.

An approach that is marketed as a compliment to exercise are "nutritional" shakes to "make sure" that you get a proper balance of nutrition. Huh? Stop wasting your money and just eat healthy good food. You have no reason to attempt to supplement your way to health. All you need is solid, good food in the right mix and calorie amount.

MYTH: You Can Exercise Your Weight Off

I'm sorry but no, you cannot. A mile on the treadmill will burn, depending on your weight, about 150 calories. After 5 miles of treadmill work, you will have approximately 650 calories burned off. (And remember – a calorie is not a calorie) While these calories are nice to get rid of, they won't necessarily lead to weight loss and if you eat (you should), the calories will be back anyway. Exercising is definitely the right thing to do – just don't do it to lose weight. Do it to be healthy. Exercise will, however, cause you to eat right and this will generally lower your body fat resulting in weight loss.

MYTH: You Can Spot Reduce

The idea that doing ab crunches will reduce the size of your belly or triceps extensions will get rid of the flab under your arms is seriously bogus. Spot reduction is a vanity-based myth that causes people to believe that the crap they hear all of the time somehow has to be true. Why would this idea be everywhere if it didn't have some truth in it?! I am sorry, but it doesn't – not even a shred. The reason that I point out the vanity-based commentary is this type of goal needs to not occur. Look at it this way: When you get healthy and stronger, you will weigh what you will weigh.

Healthy, strong, and independent should be the goals, not what is on the scale.

MYTH: No Pain, No Gain

This is a harder one to explain as it is true and not true at the same time. The definition of pain is key. If you have an acute pain in your bones, joints, or muscles, do not try to work through it. You are injured and need to seek help from either the medical community and/or a personal trainer. Basically, get with someone who knows what they are doing. Something is not right and needs to be corrected. Immediately. On the other hand, pain defined as muscle discomfort (soreness), or that occurs when you have become winded for a short time, is referring to a transition to a better you. Little to nothing good comes from your comfort zone. You need to get out of your comfort zone to make a meaningful change. Basically, if it doesn't matter, then it doesn't matter.

MYTH: If Women Lift Weights, They Will Get Bulky

In order to make this myth true, this needs to read: If women do steroids and lift weights, they may get bulky. In other words, women do not have enough testosterone to grow any serious muscle mass. I frequently get asked by women, "How do I tone?" And when I say "by lifting weights," I can see the deflated look on their face as the worry of bulking up lingers. This brings up the real issue which is vanity. Let me ask you this. If you are fit and healthy, should you really care what a spouse, friend, or even worse, a stranger may think about you? Please say no. Basically, you will not bulk up and you will struggle to get to where you want to go without resistance training.

MYTH: BMI (Body Mass Index) Determines Health

BMI refers to a ratio of height to weight and strongly suggests that there exists a singular chart covering all seven billion of us accurately. Many insurance programs and employer wellness plans are based on this premise, and higher premiums are sometimes charged to those not meeting the falsely defined criteria. The issue is that it is not accurate. The chart does OK for a larger population, but as a singular indicator of health, the chart misleads horribly. You can be skinny and of the right height and be in miserable health, but your BMI looks awesome. You can be heavier, shorter, completely muscular, and have a great cardio – basically in perfect health – but you will have a lousy BMI and find yourself paying more for insurance of suddenly seeing a nutritionist to 'help' you lose weight? Crazy!

MYTH: Your Weight Is All That Matters

Your weight is a number on a scale. We are constantly barraged with 'information' telling us that we are fat and need some new product to finally do something about it. Other factors hold a higher validity as an indicator of our health's status. Don't get me wrong, weight does matter but our A1C, blood pressure, resting heart rate, etc., are all more meaningful. My consistent argument is that if your meaningful factors are right, your weight will be right too!

Regarding weight loss as the dream: The New Year's resolution nightmare that continues year after year. As a gym owner, I've come to believe this to be a never-ending quandary where the best of intentions only lasts a few days to a few weeks. People want this year to be the one where "it" happens (whatever "it" is). Weight loss and vanity drive most of the New You verbiage, whereas health and fitness lag seriously behind with this group. We should strive from this minute on to be healthy and fit. All of our other vain aspirations will be met if we strive for healthy and fit.

A real watch-out is knowing when to listen to colleagues. Degreed or not, a lot of misinformation, while best intentioned, is distributed and can intimidate you. Women seem to be much bigger targets than men, and this silliness advances the vanity aspect of health over actual health. I've personally had people tell me that after intense training, they've lost inches, had great blood pressure, great resting heart-rate, great blood work, etc., but gain a couple of pounds and get told to stop what they're doing and start doing cardio? Seriously? This is not the time to listen. If all your numbers are awesome, your actual weight might increase. So what! Get great health and let the vanity stuff take care of itself.

MYTH: You Need to Spend Two Hours in the Gym to Get Anywhere

This is a devastating myth. Who would want this to be true? I wouldn't. The idea that time spent equals results is hogwash. Some people like the gym and enjoy the camaraderie of the place. This is awesome but does not mean that it is necessary. Get with your confidant and/or a trainer and get this timeframe down to forty-five minutes or less (including your warm-up). Please understand this point: Intensity is what drives your results, not the time in the gym. These forty-five minutes should be as intense as you can take. This needs to be a three to four days/week effort for six months. You will be surprised at what you are capable of. Please make your time matter for you.

MYTH: We All Get Too Old to Exercise

This one really wears me out. I am very unsure where the concept came from that if you are sick, injured, or old that you need rest to solve your problem. Although this is sometimes true, I will say that rest is way over-applied. I would argue that the bed and couch have disabled or killed many people at an early age. I do agree that during the time spent resting that you feel better for the moment. The issue is that you almost always made matters worse and, for some really stupid reason, more rest is the "answer" to that dilemma as well. I work really hard to make the argument that we should not die at sixty and then get buried when we are eighty. We should live until we are 79 and ¾ and get buried when we are 80. The definition of living means that we are doing what we 'want' to do until the end.

Mobility, range of motion, bone strength, muscle mass, appetite, sleep, etc., all come from exercise. Do not let age define you and if there is a cost to exercising, pay it. This is far cheaper than the hospital and way more fun too! Keep going until the last day (and then try one more). You will be glad you did.

And now to untruths that screw people up:

Something Is Better Than Nothing

Who doesn't want to hear this? While this sounds reasonable, the effect of this approach is to accomplish so little that basically nothing at all comes from it. While it is uncomfortable at first to push yourself, you will be OK. You will not only get better; you'll achieve new heights that will escape the "ease into it" fallacy. You will see results soon enough to inspire you to keep going. Results are a powerful motivator. They require some added effort but I promise, it is so worth it. This does not mean that you need to spend a long time working out. Get with a trainer and make sure that your workout is efficient. You should only need thirty minutes or so after your warm-up to complete your workout. Please understand that the point of efficiency is to also increase your intensity. These thirty minutes need to really matter. And then, get on with your day. Make this change a journey and not a destination. You are never done!

Cardio Is How You Lose Weight

Cardio = think treadmill, elliptical, etc. The math doesn't support this statement at all. A mile on the treadmill (the most efficient cardio) will burn approximately one hundred and fifty calories, and if you eat at all you will easily consume that amount. Cardio is very valuable in that it will help you increase your stamina, breathing capacity, and anaerobic threshold. It will even help you get rid of a cold! Just do not use it to lose weight. Make cardio a piece of your workout and maybe one day a week should it be your focus.

A Cheap Gym Is All You Need. They Are All the Same so Just Shop on Price

Hell, just call on the phone so you can choose without even visiting. Many, many things are wrong with this logic. It's hard to know where to start.

1. Make this a serious decision. What does price have to do with it? Please remember: YOU MATTER.
2. You should be purchasing a result and evaluating your gym to determine if they have the knowledge, motivation, and expertise to make your result happen. Nothing, and I mean nothing, is lower cost than staying healthy! The four or five hundred bucks on a gym membership is chump change compared to the costs in the medical world.
3. Cheap gyms want your money and know that you will disappear and then forget or not care that you are still being charged. Do you recognize this? Does this approach lead you to a result? Find a place that you are comfortable and the staff cares about you.
4. Boredom is a killer of motivation. Most to all of cheap gyms are cardio based with some strength equipment present to give you the concept that your goals are possible. You will get bored with the lack of options and as boredom comes, motivation goes.

5. You believe that you probably won't use it anyway so it may as well be cheap. This is serious stuff. Your success on this subject does not deserve doubt in any way. Get with your confidant and make your plan realistic so that YOUR success happens. Use your confidant's advice and ensure that your plan is solid. To which you say, "OK, I will spend lots and get there. Are you happy now?" No! The more expensive gyms have their place but tend to be niche oriented. This is fantastic if you truly have an interest in the narrowness of the offering. A valid point against this though is longevity. What you are doing is planning for a lifetime of success. To be fully satisfied with a niche product forever is taking a risk. This could be great but this is my warning to watch out. Make sure to choose a gym/activity that you can expand into and that will not lose your interest over time. A valid point is that as we get older, our ability to improve slows down. We need to accept this as a component of our choice. Our interest in the choice should not be based on the idea that we'll be the best at it. We simply need to have a very long-term liking of the activity.

The Method to Lose Weight Is Easy, I Just Need to Do It. We All Know How

Really? Does anyone honestly believe this? What I've watched and surmised is that people generally do not have any idea what they are doing. At best, they go through some motions hoping that the magic will happen to them even though it eludes the other 7 billion people who try. What is true is that we are all different and need to believe in a customized approach to our health (Hence the necessity of a confidant). As we age, have kids, buy a house, divorce, change jobs, etc., our activity levels and our nutrition change (usually dramatically), and then so does our weight, stress level, health, etc. With all of the changes that happen, the idea that "the method is easy" looks less and less easy and that is a good thing. Recognition of this difficulty is a great first step towards optimizing your healthy living approach. Get with your confidant and make a real plan that fits YOU and allows for you to change (Because you will).

Strength Machines Are the Safe Way to Get More Fit

The reality is that while strength machines are good to introduce you to strength-building movement, they do very little to improve your fitness. I see really great intentions on people's faces as they go to a piece of strength (selectorized) equipment but when they get there, the tendency is to pick the lightest weight and then do ten repetitions three times. I honestly have no idea what the real expectations are towards improvement. Nothing will happen other than wasting some time doing nothing. Picking a higher weight is difficult as the machines offer no freedom of motion to you and, therefore, you need to do it their way. The manufacturer engineers a "best fit" scenario into their design but that almost never fits you. Let the machine do its job and introduce you to a lift and take you 80% of the way there. Determine if the muscle group you are working is what you want and then ask a knowledgeable trainer to show you how to safely replicate the move with free weights. After this, ask the trainer what other options are available to enhance the move. You may be surprised at the diversity of options available to you. Be very willing to spice up your workout so you do not get bored.

If You Do a Good Workout, You Get to Do and Eat Whatever You Want

You have earned it! Nope. This is a journey. Of course you will not be perfect but spend the first six months doing your absolute best. Accept the benefits of saying no to temptation. In your past you may have chosen the temptations, even without the workout, and look where it got you. Choose to live correctly for six whopping months and learn to say no to temptation so that you succeed with your goal. After your six months of sincere effort, you will know what you can say yes to, but I encourage you to be critical of your choices so that you do not fall back into your past. As part of your new journey, you will find new acquaintances who will help to hold you accountable and while this is awesome, ultimately you are your own boss.

My Genetics Are the Cause of My Obesity or Other Health Problems

This is a bigger trap for most people as it contains some truth and for each person this truth is different. The point of me putting this statement into this chapter is to ask that you do not fall victim to the belief that no matter what you do, you will be fat, have heart disease, cancer, low testosterone, diabetic (type 2), bad eyes, etc. Some of this may be true, but you have no right to idly stand by and let these terrible occurrences happen to you. Get out and/or away from bad behavior. If you have a propensity to cancer, stay away from tobacco (first and secondhand smoke, chew, snuff). Diabetic, sugar needs to go. You do not have to eat sugar in any form. Learn yourself, plan and implement an exercise and nutrition plan that helps you with this severe problem. The same goes for heart disease and obesity. You are not a victim of your genetics but more so a victim of your environment. Take charge of your life and make the best of your issues through healthy living and THEN let the medical community assist with any leftover issues. Understand that they will see you as a customer. Do YOUR best first!

You Deserve Something

A break, a refreshment…Why? Where did that come from? Very often we want to be rewarded for just doing what we are

supposed to do. Some feel that we need a treat if we exercise at all. Did you go to work today, make your kid's lunch, go to the doctor – well then, by gosh you deserve some sort of treat. We all understand. No we don't! Where did that BS come from? You are supposed to do something of value. This is an expectation of living not some magic moment that needs recognized and rewarded. The same goes with living correctly. Your reward is good health and being fit enough to do what you want. Practically all other rewards cost money, last only a few minutes, and tend to glorify relaxation which basically has the effect of harming you. We should learn to appreciate the simplicity of life and be satisfied there. The constant barrage of comfort items that you need to buy to feel good about yourself should be evaluated through your cost/benefit lens so that you purchase what YOU truly need. I understand that we all need a treat occasionally (that's part of what makes us human), but we need to be careful to not take treats too seriously so that we focus there. Our work, family, and results matter much more than a treat.

Numeric Goals Make Tracking Success Easier

We all want to believe that if we are held accountable by a neutral device, we will behave and then succeed. Like all of these untruths, there is a nugget of reality in there, but they are not effective. The real motivator to your health needs to simply be you. Trying to appease a device by tracking steps or staying in a zone for x amount of time will lead you to not respect the device and finally to stop paying attention to it. All the while, what you needed to pay attention to is yourself. Do not get lost in the shuffle. We cannot buy our answer. We need to be our answer. If you feel the need to purchase something for motivation, join an event that is currently harder than you are capable of. This way, you have an investment that you want to pursue and a timetable to achieve this success. You win by getting ready for the event. Many events to choose from, get with your confidant and get going. Then stay going.

Healthy Living Is Boring

This can be true if you let it, but it should not be. Life should be fun and so should your health and, more importantly, your life. Enjoy the ride but, dang it, ride. This means to have challenges and that your challenges should be fulfilling and reachable. Be selective in choosing your goal so that it serves your purpose. The satisfaction received from accomplishing a goal is to drive you to the next one. Learn to accept failure as part of your journey and then laugh at it. Your goal should be reachable but not easily reachable. The mishaps will help you appreciate your successes and give you something to talk about to others who are struggling too.

Kids

Talk about a group of people that get hit from every direction. Wow! Kids cannot turn anywhere without being told that they need some new crap to be hip or happy. Clothes, food, drinks, movies, phones, games, apps – you name it – and it is thrown at these youngsters. Usually offering little to no value and asking for lots of money. Children really want to make a statement early. They want to be popular and to fit in. These desires are very normal and absolutely played upon by profiteers who "care" about the little ones.

Consider:

Myths

Juice Is a Healthy Drink

The reality is that sugar is an enemy of good health and most juice drinks contain more sugar that soda. Basically, making both really bad choices. In their natural state, a fruit's sugar content is balanced with natural fiber. When juice is made, the fiber is stripped from the fruit and only the sugar moves on into the drink. 100% fruit juice sounds healthy, but it's not. It's sugar water. Parents should take the opportunity at an early age to "change the game" and not create a sugar-based diet. Our sugar dependency is learned, not natural.

Kids Need a Structured Exercise Program

No – kids need to play. Period. Outside or inside. Let them play. Their inventive minds will get them into and out of a lot of trouble. They will learn what they're capable of and what boundaries to push. You are right, they might get banged up, but the overall benefits cannot be understated. We all claim to not want our children to be captivated with screens but this cannot be mandated in this day and age. We have to allow alternatives that they want. Play is a great answer. The magnetic pull of the screen is real and will someday takeover but ultimately their fun will come from doing something and not watching something. Be willing to plant the seed. It may not grow but plant it anyway.

Untruths

We Have to Start Technology Early So Our Kids Do Not Fall Behind

Technology will always change; you cannot stop it. Therefore, jump in anytime and learn from there. Kids will learn it from somewhere, don't worry. Your job as a parent is to teach kids to be healthy and active. The technology stuff will happen on its own.

Kids Don't Like Healthy Food

Do not be afraid to turn the tide. If they have been conditioned to eat crap (and you eat crap too), then make it a project to change. Keep your goals out in front of everyone so that all are on board. Have a discussion and listen to their concerns and accommodate where you can, but MAKE THE CHANGE! Everyone wins. Feeling better is a great goal! Being healthier is the goal. Do this!

Now, the real question: How do I do this? And here is an opportunity to put your previous efforts to good use. You use the Good Food Items (GFI) that you created earlier and apply it to you and your family. Find good foods that everyone likes and eat it. Pretty simple. Now try to add to the list on a weekly basis so that you have more variety to choose from. Don't get too rigid on the content of the list. Anything that is good food that someone likes should land on the list, but make sure to keep the list's integrity high.

Also, make sure to have fun as a family with your meals. Good food is good food. There isn't any reason to make someone eat something they do not like. If you like it, you eat it. Don't worry about them, and they will be alright. Their approval may come later and that is awesome. Take the long view.

Pre-teens and Teenagers don't like to exercise

As with anyone, fun is the answer. During the pre-teen years, get them involved. Find something they like and see that they pursue the activity. This is an era where team sports prevail, which is great, but anything they like that is active will work. Make something happen. You'll be glad you did. Then work to instill independence and pursuit of excellence in your child. Accept that we are not all the same and have different strengths. Success to this age group is important. Find what they like and help them succeed. This should transition them into the teen years.

During the teen years, pick up where you left off in the pre-teen years. They still don't like to exercise (Myth and Untruth – refuting this is up to you). Keep refining the choices to play to your kid's strengths and likes. There are no right or wrong activities other than no activity. Everyone should do something productive. This is a total judgment-free zone. Keep the long view and work to instill the value of health – nutrition and exercise – on both fronts. I have no doubt that this era will be weird with a nice mix of frustrations. We all go through this. I'll say it again – keep the long view.

The one watch-out that I would like to discuss in this age group is the possible differences between team activities and individual activities. Team activities are more popular. They offer camaraderie, teach team building skills, leadership skills, and the value of your input into a larger picture. If you have a bad day on the team and someone has a great day and picks up your slack, awesome – it's all good. The downside to team activities relates to after the season is over. You decide not to participate next season or you graduate. What then? What I tend to see is a plunge in motivation regarding staying active. Without the team atmosphere to propel you to new heights, being active tends to lose its shine. And while this is not a guaranteed outcome, it does happen more than it doesn't.

Individual activities lack the depth of the advantages listed in the team activities. They are there, just not predominant. What they can create is a self-motivated self-improvement mindset that has an increased likelihood of carrying over into adulthood. In an individual sport (cross-country, track, golf, tennis, gymnastics, swimming, etc.), the participant creates their own finish. The motivation to improve comes from seeing yourself go to the next level. If you hit your PR (personal record), the glory is yours. If you don't do well, you get to eat it. The ability to internalize the responsibility of success leads to an understanding that success and/or failure rests on your shoulders. What you eat, how you sleep, practice, strategize, etc., is yours. In the end, your result is yours alone. These participants go forward into life knowing that the future they create is the one they will live in. The better they do, the better they do.

Both approaches to teen years have merits and faults, and I fully encourage you to get your child into something. Sitting on the sidelines and waiting for something good to happen will lead to serious disappointment and it may take decades to change directions. While the teen years are important, we need to realize that they are over with when you hit twenty and if you live to eighty, this is only twenty-five percent of your life. Each and every year is unto itself and needs to be considered important. You matter! Do not let time go by. Today is your day!

Conclusion: This chapter is a little hard to write as there is so much "information" out there that is pure BS. My hope is that you thoroughly evaluate each influence that you let into your fitness life. Your plan should include unbiased research before implementing ANY plan. If your discovery includes promises of lowering weight or improving vanity, then be very wary. If your discovery uncovers a need to spend money on stuff, be very wary. If your discovery gives ANY timetable for success, be very wary.

Basically, what I am stating is that you know that you need a comprehensive plan that includes nutrition management and hard work that last you from now onward. You are smart enough to be skeptical. Please be willing to do so.

It's very little wonder that health and fitness take a back seat for kids. The misinformation, air-brushed photos, vanity nonsense that they need to endure is frightening. The parents' role in better preparing the next generation for what's ahead of them cannot be overstated. Healthcare costs will continue their meteoric rise, and the need to be healthy will be even more important. False information will only grow as the value of health becomes apparent. People will always be chasing an easy dollar. Don't give it to them. Your health and your children's health is too important.

I cannot overemphasize the real impact of these untruths as the average person will believe some of this stuff and when it doesn't become true, will lose motivation, and believe that there isn't anything they can do to get the results desired. If/when this happens, I could not be sorrier nor angrier. YOU MATTER!

Chapter Three
Social Circle

How does our social circle affect our choices?

I'm going to start with a testimonial from Melissa. This is a textbook perfect attitude towards self-care that, while understanding real life, values a longer view of life and a willingness to explore a new venue that fits her where she is. Life takes twists and turns and so should you.

From Melissa:

Being active is always something I did. It is my way of managing my persistent low-grade anxiety. And I have enough vanity to want to remain thin. I have also experienced enough personal turmoil to have periods when I felt a bit lost or that there is a void in my life. Transitions in life can bring about a lack of direction and some loneliness and boredom. So, in January of 2015, I was divorced, had recently moved, and had a 1-year-old daughter. Working as a deputy prosecuting attorney, I had a busy schedule, and decided the only way I could continue to get regular exercise was during my work day lunch hours. Over the years, I had done a variety of different activities. I biked when I lived near the bike trail. I went to fitness classes and a boxing gym when I lived in the city.

Before my daughter was born, I was active with my flamenco dance group. I walked a lot. I tried running, but never liked it. At this point, I decided to join a gym very near my office so I could be active on my lunch hour. I started out light. I hadn't done much in a while. I would get on the elliptical, run on the treadmill, row on the rowing machine. I was looking at workouts online to create a circuit training course to incorporate some light weight and variety. The gym was nice. The lunch hour was working well for me. It was going ok.

Then I was invited to a "Bust It" class. (Build Up Strength Through Intensive Training). I had met the coach (and gym owner) before. We met at a career fair in town. He was there as a business owner and personal trainer. I was there with the prosecutor's office. We chatted. I told him I was running a Rugged Maniac (Obstacle Course Race). He immediately signed up to run it too. I asked about his work. I had an interest in fitness. So, we had an already established rapport and respect for one another.

It was the first class. I had no idea what I was doing. I did not know what Bust It was. I had never ever lifted free weights with a barbell. I didn't know anything about form or technique. I didn't know where or what my "traps" were. I was kind of scared of lifting weights. What if I drop it and hurt myself? I didn't understand the Bust It terminology. I asked, "When will we do this work-out again?"

He said, "Never." I didn't understand that; other than some benchmark workouts, the workout would be different every day. After the first week, I was so sore I was walking funny. I learned a few lifts. I started with very light weight. My first power clean was 45 pounds.

Dave was a fantastic coach – a great teacher. I was learning the techniques, the philosophies, the theories, the movements. He was supportive, yet he pushed me harder than I had ever been pushed. My confidence was soaring through the roof. My body was transforming. The classes were SO FUN. Small classes, but others learning like I was. We cheered each other on and commiserated about our aches and pains. For this hour during the day, the whole world was shut out. No law. No cases. No anxieties. There was just me and the bar. In the workout area, I had to be extremely focused on what I was physically doing, and that shut down my mind of all other thoughts. It was therapeutic.

Of course, I would go back to the office and get back to work. I would pick up my daughter after work and parent. I was looking for a new home and dealing with all the stresses of life. But I would carry the thoughts of my workout with me throughout the day. I would feel the wonderful tightness of my muscles. I would sleep easily and deeply because my body was exhausted. I looked forward to the next day's workouts. The challenges, seeing my classmates. My confidence was building. I felt physically and mentally stronger and more confident. It added some adventure and excitement and fun in my life to be reaching deadlift PR. It was so fun and empowering. I was hooked.

There are not many influences that impact our choices more than those we love and trust. Establishing a group enables like-minded people to step in and support a healthy lifestyle for all. Melissa references the impact of her classmates and coach as positive and helpful to her in keeping her challenged and interested. This atmosphere enables her to relieve stress, build a healthier body, and share time with like-minded people. Again, this is textbook perfect and will lead to her best possible result.

We as a society strive to keep these people confident that we belong in their inner circle and vice-versa. On many different fronts, these dynamic serves all well: church, school, kids, etc. They are your "go to" people. You go to them and they come to you.

So, why would you mess this up? Sometimes our inner circle isn't the most beneficial to our needs. The uncomfortable truth is that the norm is overweight and unhealthy, and anything you do that is against the "norm" will cause resistance. If you are successful and fit, people will envy you. Even those who love you will resent you. Don't let them sabotage you.

Therefore, sometimes we need to be honest with ourselves and accept that things could be better and that we want them to be. If you're not sleeping well, are overweight, lack energy, smoke, struggle with simple things, maybe you need to adjust your lifestyle more than a little bit. Having a long-term view of your life means that you need to create, to the best of your ability, an ideal circumstance. This evolution may take years. Let it! Move at a pace that gets you to where you need to go. Balance is key to keeping YOUR circle together. Try not to do anything drastic as the pushback has a higher chance of overwhelming you and getting you off track. This isn't worth it. Your winning long-term is paramount to your success.

What is needed is a "silo" mindset that singles out your core belief, leaving it unaltered by others' opinions. You pretty well know that you want to be stronger, faster, weigh less, have more energy and the like. These are core values that get compromised by what? Opinions or priorities of others? Why?

We are programmed to believe that others' needs matter more than ours, and then if we look at it differently, then we're just selfish. I'm going to argue against this point by stating reality. If you take care of yourself, you will have MORE energy, be sick LESS, be STRONGER and FASTER, and ultimately LESS selfish because you can do MORE.

Isn't that awesome? And it's TRUE. Is this new to you? Is this information that you've been waiting for?

I'm encouraging you to be solid in your beliefs. Build a backbone and stop the BS. Do you like living? Yes. Do you like being healthy? Yes. Do you think that eating chemicals or fast food are good for you? No. Then act on it!

What does "build a backbone" mean? I have a backbone now. What are you talking about? I'm tough, big, and bad! Really – look around. If you are, you're a rarity. What are you missing?

Is exercise good for you? Then do it.

Are you too good for fast food? Yep. I am.

Be OK with these.

A decision matrix is useful to assist you with the obvious. This doesn't have to be complicated (and it shouldn't be either).

Decision Matrix*		
	Question	Answer – Yes/No
1	Am I overweight?	
2	Am I diabetic?	
3	Do I have hypertension?	
4	Am I stressed?	
5	Do I lack energy?	

*If these questions aren't appropriate, develop your own. These five took about two minutes to come up with. Yours needs to be relevant to you.

If you answer yes to any of the questions, then it's time to evaluate your lifestyle and develop a solution.

If you choose to not change direction, please answer (to yourself) – why not? Then evaluate that answer and determine if your answers honestly make sense. If they do not, please do not overlook them and just go on. This only perpetuates the problem.

After these thought processes are complete, make the appropriate changes and recognize that not all changes will have enough effect to matter. You need to choose appropriately for your situation and interest. Your confidant can help you determine if your chosen route is sufficient to "move the needle." Please listen to him or her. You are the ultimate beneficiary of any change. Make it matter. Also, self-evaluate. So that changes can be made to suit you. Run the idea by your confidant so that the effectiveness is still there, but feel free to change it up to suit you! This is liberating for you. This is your life we're talking about. Use it!

All changes of any significant measure begin within your personal circle. You should expect support or difficulties there first. What do you do? If you get full support, you become grateful and make everyone proud of you. Include them on your journey and find bonding opportunities that all can participate in like hiking, biking, or cooking. Enjoy the growth that is occurring.

If you get less than full support, do not ignore it. You need to gauge the severity of the resistance. First, understand that change is scary and that others may feel that you are being judgmental towards them. Second, you need to allay these feelings and make this about your goal to improve yourself. The "how you got where you're at" is irrelevant. You love them and only want to become the best version of yourself. Third, everyone wins and you should show everyone the benefits you're planning and over-communicate them so as to leave no doubt of their inclusion. Third, try to get other family members on board with you. Let any takers begin with baby steps. Any self-improvement on anyone's part is to be congratulated as they all move towards acceptance.

When the advice you are seeking only slightly deviates from yours, you easily adjust or explain away the differences. No one gets upset and things go well. There might be a small discussion, but almost everyone will allow you latitude to make a decision affecting your life.

Now what happens when this social circle gets challenged? What happens when you decide to become "different" than they are used to? If the changes are not positive (and you know it – drugs, eating disorder, alcohol, infidelity, etc.), you would hope for an intervention that prevents further damage and holds you accountable to fix the situation.

When the change is positive but doesn't go too far, you can pretty much count on the support of the group. You might get some looks and stuff but overall – approval. One thing to watch out for is "advice" from well-meaning friends regarding working out. Usually their priorities revolve around protein and weight loss. Things like, "Surely you're not getting enough protein?" and, "How much weight are you planning to lose?" Neither of these really matter. Eat well and don't care about weight loss, and you will be fine.

This same strategy applies towards the next layer of friends and acquaintances. But if they're in the next layer, accept only their support. Any negativity needs to be politely listened to and then immediately discarded.

You do need to be resolute with your plan, but don't shove your opinion in anyone's face. A guard will go up and you will feel judged until you quit and then beat up for quitting. Understand that most in society don't care about you at all. This is liberating! You're free to be healthy. Just think about how you project yourself so that you enjoy the new you and don't alienate others. Your goal is to get them to follow along with you.

Let's start at the beginning. What is the change that we are referring to?

The change that I am speaking to revolves around the idea that you are accepting a challenge that will leave you with a better you. You are no longer satisfied with your approach to life and want a better outcome. While this sounds like everyone would obviously be for it, that's not quite the case and you know it, and are worried about it.

What happens when the change you are embarking on is for you? What might you expect? What should you do?

All of us are at different points in our journey. Some are already healthy-minded, some are in transition, and some are just starting to consider becoming healthier. Each group reacts to others criticism differently. Let's chase these concepts and see where they go.

What happens when the change is positive, but doesn't go too far?

The Already Healthy-Minded Adult:

If you are already a healthy-minded adult, this won't be hard. If those in this group want to ramp up their workout or to delete/add a food group, acceptance is pretty easy. You might hear "What?" and "Why?" but just about any reasonable answer will relieve the situation. You might get mocked or made fun of, but you are used to it and generally let it slide. No harm, no foul. This group is generally accepted as is. They might be considered "kooky" at worst but they are considered to know what they're doing so no problem.

Adults in transition to become healthy minded:

Several around you are vocally noticing that you are taking this healthy thing seriously and are feeling threatened. The number of naysayers probably exceeds positive people five to one. It won't take too much to convince them that you ARE serious this time. Get with your confidant very early on to make sure that you message your goals so as not to alienate anyone. This is your goal, and it shouldn't take too much to head off any negative commentary. Understand that your success is paramount to anyone's feelings but if it doesn't take too much to accommodate everyone, then my advice is to make everyone comfortable. They may even take your enthusiasm to heart and begin their own improvement program. The folks in this group will get a lot of questions regarding motive, and you will have to understand that the generally accepted reason for becoming healthy is to lose weight. I really don't like to say this but: Don't argue that you're trying to get healthy and not worried about the weight. You would be better off beating your head on a brick wall. Keep your sanity and understand that you are at a fragile point in your journey. Useless arguments like this one may cause you to revert to the self that you were trying to leave. The serious naysayers will need to be placated so they leave you alone. If you give them an opening, they will seize on the opportunity and work to drive you back into your old self so they feel better about themselves. Be determined and focus on you. Do not let their comments divert you.

Adults considering becoming healthy:

This group is fragile and susceptible to commentary from peers. This group will have to develop a tight alliance with a strong and proven health-minded person. You will need their strength to step into your fray for you and fend off the negativity. This negativity can come in the form of mockery, laughter, snickering, doubts, etc. You know the "C'mon, be serious," and "Again, really?" This talk is tough to take. Here is what you do: Accept that you are fragile. It's OK! What this means is that you NEED a confidant who is sincere. Talk to them often and let them know of ANY concerns you have regarding the status of your journey. Your seriousness at this point is paramount to your success. You do not have to be self-reliant, but your sincerity is needed. The right confidant will steer you back on track and explain what is honestly going on. Usually the commentators are self-reflecting. Their comments have little to nothing to do with you and more with them. Their non-stated goal is to drag you down so that you return to the unhappy person you were before, and that the community hierarchy is left as it was. This is a tough hill to climb and will take your strong character and determination to keep your eye on the prize. This group needs to have a series of short-term goals that can be achieved and then showcased and celebrated. For this group, another quarter mile on the treadmill is a win, another pound lost is a win, dropping soda from your diet is a win. Encouragement is needed on all levels and continued until an honest desire to get healthy sticks. These folks would benefit from getting into a group class where camaraderie is valued and successes communally enjoyed. Take pride in others' successes, and see yourself reaching new heights as well. Your genuine happiness will be appreciated, and you will receive appreciation in kind. Motivation needs to come from all angles so you keep your focus. If you are the friend of someone transitioning, recognize this opportunity and take pride in being selected. Be a solid supporter of this person, and help them be encompassing in their journey. Inform them that it's OK they didn't work out today, they can do this tomorrow, but they need to use today to move their needle forward. Give up soda. Give up fast food. Sleep eight hours. Put the cell phone down. In other words, make this a multifaceted journey and that each and every front is critically important to the overall result. As a friend, support any and all of these wins. They are looking to you to help them and you should do so.

What happens when there is a dramatically positive change (such as total physical health transformation)?

Healthy minded adults:

This group is evidently looking to get out of a trap. These folks have moved to a new situation and have decided to make a drastic change to their inner circle. Probably something negative has happened (divorce, forced job change, leaving an addiction, etc.) and a sincere desire to start over takes hold.

Positive steps are always welcome, and I would encourage this group to seek that one person or group who they admire and trust to keep this going. It is very difficult for an individual to follow through on their own change. We come to adulthood with an individualized ethos and honestly, it's hard to break. Whatever your past has brought you will be hard to negate without help. Take your time and find the right person/group to carry you forward so that you CANNOT retract. Understand that this is an awesome change you're making and put a personal infrastructure in place to sustain it. You are worth it.

Adults transitioning to being healthy minded:

This group will have the propensity to start out hard and think they "have it figured out!" They'll lose the pounds, pump the pecs, and be on their way. They got this! Slow down. Take the long view, and realize that this is a journey and not a destination. This rapid, perfect living can be easy to derail and will yield great results while you're at it. When you stop, for any reason, you'll find it hard to start again. Learn to take a solid approach to your health so that you are sure to sustain it. Get a confidant and develop a long-term strategy.

Adults considering being healthy:

Beginning with a dramatic shift is probably not the approach for you. Many steps need to be in place before you move to this hardcore approach if you're considering taking the step. It is very unlikely that you're ready to go all out. Get with a confidant or an awesome personal trainer and develop a long-term plan to succeed. Your attitude is going the right direction, and I'm very glad for you. Be smart and take the time to be successful. You are worth it!

Conclusion

Your social circle has a huge influence on you. We don't exactly pick our social circle, and that is for the better.

Our family and friends are a crazy mix of people we are around and so be it. What is needed is a will and a mechanism to make being healthy acceptable to this group so they can support you in their own best way. Use a simple matrix and develop a solid plan.

If you are currently a healthy-minded person, chances are that anything you do toward keeping yourself where you are will be fully accepted. Your circle will identify you as "one of them" and you can you go your merry way towards a fitter you! Congratulations! Your interest will stay high, and they will have lots to talk about. Maybe they'll even join you?

If your social circle is less supportive and shares their lack of enthusiasm with you, then you need to make up the difference. You have a choice at this point to either argue your case (results of the matrix) or discard the comments of the naysayers. Discover a trusted confidant! You need to win. Kinda simple, really.

What about kids who are healthy-minded?

First off, all kids are vulnerable. All of them. Be diligent to not allow anything to thwart them. As adults and mentors to our children and other kids who look up to us, we need to ensure we carefully encourage and invoke a physically healthy mindset into our children. We are surrounded with pressure to raise the perfect child and drive them into developing a skill that others appreciate. Think of dancing, singing, band, education, baseball, football, basketball, etc.

What about the kid? What do they want? This is where the parent needs to practice active listening and then provide opportunities for success. Now – after you have done all of that – know that the child will still be subjected to mean-spirited talk from peers who want to know what you're doing in their group. If you are not veering too far from your child's current interests, you can expect success. If the kid wants to move into a new direction, let them. Find where they want to go, and help them succeed. Remember to be glad they are choosing a direction and guide them to success. You may or may not know what to do to help and that's OK. Learn what is needed. Evaluate your competency to help and then fill in the holes. Be picky with the kid, but supportive. Many kids want to start at the top and go from there. Help them to understand that in order to succeed, they need to learn the ropes and listen to those who have made it. Their learning this feat will help them with whatever they want to approach. Remember: They do not have years of mess-ups to guide them in an approach. That's what parents are for.

What about kids who are transitioning to a healthy lifestyle?

Remember that kids are vulnerable. All of them. At this point in their life, they are smarter than we know. They understand that healthy means eating right, exercising, and accomplishing goals that matter. They are not tied up with career or life nonsense. They can focus on themselves, and we should encourage them to do so. When they are concerned about our food supply being unhealthy (it's pretty freaking bad), acknowledge they're right and take an active interest in accurate education and information. This is a bonding moment opportunity. Don't pass it up. For exercise, find out what they are thinking and make sure they are outfitted for success. This doesn't mean that you have to spend a fortune. Good shoes, good shorts, good shirt, keep them hydrated, and you're off! The necessities will come up. Accommodate them to the best of your ability and watch the flower bloom. Again, this is a bonding time. Make the most of it, and you will treasure this time the rest of your life. Kids will have plenty of necessary diversions to occupy their time and choices will have to be made. It will involve one activity winning and another losing. This is the continuum of being a parent. It is understandable that healthy living will take a backseat periodically; however, being a parent involves ensuring that the right pathway is returned to as soon as possible. When these circumstances come up, you have to understand that your child is vulnerable at this point and in serious need of parenting to efficiently return them to the right path. Make this transition as fun as you can, but make it happen!

What about kids who are considering being healthy minded?

I'm completely serious about this point, so I will state it again. Kids are vulnerable. This group more than ever. What we adults need to consider is that these kids are probably being bullied on some level and have to struggle with negative thoughts. Regardless, if your child comes to you wanting to change, your first response is to listen. Discover the root cause. Discover if they are being bullied or if they just want better. Then help determine if the solution presented will get the kid where they need to be. This moment can be the most important in a child/parent relationship. They have opened a window of opportunity for you, and now you need to do your best. This is the predicament that I dream of with people in general. To have your own kid come to you and ask for help with life –

priceless! Please note that this situation is real, and I am grateful for your foresight to help them. The strategy here is twofold. The first is to help them identify some short-term success and then DO NOT DROP THE BALL. Provide the venue that will bring your child to the best level they are capable of in an arena that they choose. Teach them to see over their own hill and that their future is theirs and worth going after. Make sure to note that your child's fun and success is paramount. Being a parent is a major responsibility, and your job just got easier! The watch-outs for this group are real as well. Do not underestimate the vulnerability of these kids. They do NOT want to fail. Be willing to see that they reach their dreams but sit down with them and create a pathway to victory. If they want to play softball but never have before, take them to an automated batting cage. Sure this does not mimic real life, but the ice is broken. Golf – go to a driving range. Tennis – take them to the park and throw balls at them to hit. Running – go to the track. Nothing bad can happen and trying again is easy. Keep it positive and keep it fun. Flex from beginning to end with the caveat that quitting is only possible when a replacement becomes available. If your child loved the idea of tennis and now does not, then its tennis until an option is chosen to explore (i.e. softball, running, Frisbee). Be in it to win it!

If your social circle is actively not supportive, then this puts a large burden on you as the parent to "go against the grain," and make your child's healthy lifestyle and involvement in activity a success. Your engagement in being active and healthy-minded is paramount to your kids at this point. They need to see you live a healthy life! It is a shame that your social circle doesn't consider the benefits of activity but that doesn't get you off the hook. You actually need to work harder to make a difference. You being an involved parent will be greatly appreciated by your child.

This is also a case where your activity level helps to empower your argument that your kids need to be as involved as possible in positive events so they can reap the rewards of success. Show them that their choices now will help determine their future tomorrow. Nothing will happen if nothing is tried. Be a leader and make your children self-supportive through activities and watch their self-esteem grow – along with their successes. Creating a healthy lifestyle at this point in their journey will help them throughout life. Be an agent of this support!

Kids are always going to be vulnerable. The good thing about a social circle in this arena is that they're generally supportive of kids doing the right thing. If this is your case, awesome, and expand on it. Get others involved in your kid's success so that they feel the love. Being active yourself will help your argument that great things build great things. Let it!

Chapter Four
Self-Esteem

Did you ever wonder why some people take care of themselves and some do not? Some dig deep into their lives to ensure they choose healthy choices on all fronts, some choose to create a façade to cover various lapses of judgment, and some do not seem to care at all. Why? These descriptions describe opposing lifestyle choices. Your personal self-esteem causes your behavior. Our plan is to describe these attitudes so that you can see yourself in one (or in a combination) of these definitions, then set the goal of making the best choices for yourself.

Healthy Self-Esteem

This is the person that we most want everyone to see us as. This person understands the difficulties that we face on a constant basis and chooses to overcome them. These people have little fear that they will be judged poorly and that their efforts will yield a better person for themselves and those around them. These people see a physical or mental goal, discover what it takes to succeed, and start moving that direction. Money is sometimes necessary and so be it. Sometimes they understand that they will look disjointed as they move forward. They reject the judgment and mockery they will encounter from folks who do not understand the value nor purpose of their goal. To have a healthy self-esteem means to "be truly comfortable in your own skin." Most everyone falls short of this goal as we do care what others think of us. We know that we are doing the right things but when we get those looks or snide comments, we cave and want to be considered "normal." We have watched reckless comments sidetrack dreams too often.

What we miss when we see these people are the struggles and self-doubts they go through. These folks are inundated with messaging that their efforts are misguided and that they need to purchase something – new shoes, outfits, supplements, protein powder, the right kind of protein powder, etc. These people constantly need to rebut rumors and falsehoods.

Women seem to take the brunt of the negativity for trying to take themselves seriously and to work on their fitness. Often they are told that lifting weights will make them bulky and that men won't like that.

1. Women do not produce enough testosterone to develop nor support bulky muscles. They never will either. This is just a fact of life.
2. The people making the comments that strong women will not be liked usually have severe self-esteem issues of their own and need to mind their own business. Active women are strong and need supported and modeled after – not knocked down.

The next comment that we hear toward those that are seriously trying is that they are skinny enough. Wait, what? The point of working out is only to get skinny? That should be at the bottom of the list. Weight management is a "side effect" of fitness. Don't worry about it. Secondly: Getting healthy and better is to be the goal, not skinny – whatever that is.

Here is a comment from a client with a great perspective:

"After a few months of weight-lifting, I weighed myself and realized I had gained 10 lbs.! I weighed more than I had ever weighed. I told my coach, and he gave me a high five! It was a moment of realization. I was fitter than ever, my waist was smaller, and my body fat had decreased. My thinking about weight forever changed."

Everyone needs this attitude.

For guys – the comments seem to be the reverse of those toward women. Men are told to bulk up and look big. Make sure that they are taking the full array of supplements. Big muscles are what make you fit.

1. Cardiovascular and respiratory systems are a far better determinant of health than muscle size. As the heart and lungs are on the inside of your body, people can't see them and only remark on what they can see, i.e. muscles. This is not a valid way to determine fitness. Become a whole package and muscles will develop as well. Our question for you:

What is more important to you at 2 AM – your bicep or your heart? Which should you prioritize?

2. Supplements are just that – supplements. Most are not needed in any aspect as your nutrition management should cover your true needs. If they do not, re-evaluate your nutrition until it does. You will save money and have better results too.

Both genders are told that genetics are the real source of weight management and fitness.

1. We all basically have the same genetics that the caveman did and that was millions of years ago.
2. Those with strong and healthy self-esteem have lives that are full of missteps and struggles. They just work through them and reap their benefits. Doing the right thing is hard but these folks are diligent enough to succeed.

And in all fitness-based endeavors, we are told that we are crazy and that we should just focus on enjoying life? The answer is: "We are!" The people telling us to "enjoy life," as though we are not, tend to be "comfortable" where they are and wonder why you don't join them? Life to these people revolve around themselves and includes the perception that there isn't anything that can be done to help ourselves so why try? In their eyes, we are who we are and should be happy with that. In contrast, those with a healthy self-esteem are happy with themselves but know that they can get better and choose to enjoy the challenges they face and even create challenges to overcome. Those with a healthy self-esteem are willing to step into situations that are unlikely to go perfectly, and they are OK with that.

The people telling us to question ourselves usually have self-esteem issues and choose to believe marketing campaigns touting "loving ourselves," and then defining happiness to include consuming their stuff. Those with a healthy self-esteem choose to define their own happiness and see the connection between choices and outcomes.

The people who question you also tend to believe that spending on fitness is a luxury and that most cannot afford it. To them, money spent on fitness is an unnecessary extravagance. This mindset goes back to the idea that we do not have any control of our health and we need to "save" money. Cutting this healthy nonsense is a no-brainer to them. The realities are far from this belief, but those with a healthy self-esteem are inundated with this negativity. We choose to go against the tide and to do what is right. The benefits include a healthier you, a more motivated circle of friends, active and non-active options (it's now your choice), and lower health care costs. All of this combined with a higher standard of living, more awareness of what is going on around you, an increased willingness to say "malarkey" to promises of an easy answer, less stress, higher energy, etc. The list of benefits is too numerous to mention, but you need to believe that you are in charge of your health and are wise to choose correctly. My comment and advice to those with a healthy self-esteem: You're awesome and keep going!

Facade Based Self-Esteem

This is the person who seeks lifestyle improvements on primarily an ascetic front. These folks are trying to look good on the outside and to gain approval of all acquaintances. This behavior is based on "looking" the part, and are usually on a diet of some sort, tans, pretends that something is better than nothing, wants to be better and then done with the process. These folks will follow the commercial messaging that they need "something" to be successful.

Façade based self-esteem people will live a yo-yo lifestyle where they "need" external motivation to get them going. Their usual buzzwords include: "This is the year," "I'm serious this time," "I just want to be skinny," "I need to lose weight," etc. I've seen this crowd do this: They'll check the scale when they arrive at the club, then they'll walk (not run, but walk) on the treadmill for twenty minutes, get off, and go back to the scale. Really?

Having said that, we do applaud the intensity of their effort. We feel sympathy towards them as they are destined to fail. It is very hard to understate the need for correct motivation and know the cruelty of people striving for the status quo. The wish for easy answers is killing these people.

Façade based self-esteem folks have trouble seeing the connection between their efforts and their health.

1. While we understand that this group may think that there is a difficulty connecting your efforts and your health, there isn't! The connection is real, and deep, and forever. To doubt this is to value wasting time

(which no one does). Get with a confidant, develop a sincere plan to improve your health, and believe that the skinny, new you will happen when your priorities are set straight (Confidants are extremely important as they can be awesome sounding boards for you to get and stay on the right track. I believe them to be important enough that we have a chapter dedicated to them.)

2. Do not lose time. Some people struggle with the comment in point 1 for years (some forever) and only succeed in making a valuable transformation harder. You are never too late to succeed. Your level of success will change if you wait, but you will be better. Your improvements are yours and worth achieving. Again, get with your confidant and make this happen! You are worth being healthy for you. Hurry up and do so. The vanity stuff that you worry about will get fixed in the process. Also, it is very important to have a healthy definition of success. Success can be as simple as being able to do something that you haven't been able to do for a long time. I often use this example: I want to be able to climb a tree well into my seventies. I may choose not to, but I want to be able to.

3. Take a serious look at your nutrition management. If you have vanity concerns, there is a high probability that your nutrition is not in control.

First, discover why you are focused on vanity. This is a Y in the road moment for you. Trust me, the vanity component will happen to those committed to a healthful change in their lives. To those whose primary focus is vanity-based: you will struggle to find any success at all.

Our hope is that you are heading off the vanity train wreck and onto being fitness-minded. Know that you will have residual bad habits that will be hard to break. Line them up and knock them down. Sugar is a difficult culprit to eliminate but reducing will greatly help. Processed foods – if the ingredient list has an item that you cannot pronounce, put it back. There is a lot of hidden sugar in beverages. Juices and soda should be left on the shelf. Sleep – strive to create a foundation that allows for eight hours. A foundation is important as it is repeatable. Exercise – get with your confidant, get a plan, and be diligent! Your minimum goal should be two-and-a-half hours of honest exercise per week.

4. Do not try to micromanage your fitness. Live a fit and healthy life. The rest will work itself out. Far too often this group feels the need to look the part and try to make all efforts look easy and effortless. Stop that! We change constantly and, what may have worked before, may not now. We know that we want this to be simple, and it is, just not at the beginning. Your sincerity towards a healthy lifestyle will help determine the time it takes for this to be easy. The more sincere you are, the easier and faster your transformation will be. We promise you. This means that you'll have to sweat. Understand that fitness is hard and if you do not climb into the unknown, there is little chance of your success. It's OK, and a little fun, to feel silly trying something

new. How far can you go on a standing long jump? Find out! You should get qualified help to make sure that you are safe, but if you don't get it on the first try, don't give up, and laugh a little. It's tremendously OK to "fail." Believe in yourself and you will succeed.

A very big point for this group is to have fun. View this transformation as a journey and then enjoy it. Get with your confidant and bake fun into your workout. In the beginning, fun should consume over half of your workout. You should analyze your day's plan and if it doesn't have fun included, then figure out why and then change it. If you need a group, classes are great. The folks in classes will instantly like you and pull for you. Understand that they are very happy that you are there. Your vanity bent will go away when you discover that you all suck (at the class) and that no one cares. This effort is for you and you alone! Enjoy it.

Those Who Do Not Care at All.

For various reasons, there are people who believe that they are who they are and that we should be OK with that. These folks do not see a direct connection between their physical selves and their personal success and/or feel helpless in succeeding at change – so, why? This behavior is somewhat based on the prioritization of other aspects in their lives to call successful. The belief is that career success, perceived common sense and wisdom, pricey toys, etc., will be considered more valuable than their health. They believe that their health is genetically determined with little they can do anyway. Those that do not care at all have a condescending outlook. They will be interested in their own creature comforts and of those around them. Poor fitness enablers surround these folks and incite them to sit down, relax, and rest when the opposite is what needs to be told to them. To this group, getting sick and going to the doctor for the "solution" just makes sense. Doctors are the expert, right? The positive side of these folks is that their stress is usually less as they spend minimal time on self-improvement which allows more time for leisure. This might not be the best way to spend time but their stress is less. To convince this group to value their health and to take responsibility for it will take a major mind shift. Self-esteem is currently measured by others' approval and as long as they're "nice," all is OK. Not true but this demographic can get away with it – that is until they can't. The frustrating point is that when these people's health begins to fall apart (and it will), the stress level that was minimized earlier is still sought after and the only way to continue at this level is to lower expectations (i.e. make everything easier and basically "lower the bar" on life). The approval from earlier times converts to sympathy – which is nice – but only accomplishes further harming the recipient's health and teaches those around them what to expect if they don't take care of themselves. Blind approval leading to sympathy.

What should be done about this group?

1. Education: This group needs to discover that their health is mostly in their hands. Improvements can and do happen. The sooner they start, the better they will do. Another big point regarding education:

Weight loss needs relegated to its proper place. While it's nice to lose weight, your weight will take care of itself when you live well. To just focus on the scale is serious mistake. Live well, become strong and as agile as you can, and your weight will not be a problem.

2. Responsibility: This group needs to understand that the choice to be healthy is theirs and theirs alone. Healthcare in this country is very expensive. Insurance companies are discovering options to refuse coverage and, at a minimum, increasing costs. If this group doesn't want to be a part of this dilemma, they need to accept their own health as their responsibility.

3. Encouragement: This group needs constant encouragement to get on board with the healthier minded people. These folks do not innately feel accepted. In some respects, these folks would like to just disappear and not matter. Self-esteem issues are rampant. They do matter and need to be encouraged from their beginning and even through the point where they are independent. The ups and downs that we face in our journey are perfectly normal, but can be devastating to those who are coming onboard.

4. Opportunity: This group needs the opportunity to make the needed change. Fun is a necessary component of anyone's transformation and quality opportunities can provide this. Our belief is that a "perfect" opportunity would be one that several choose to do with most completing the task

effortlessly. The one who is struggling has a light bulb moment and realizes that he/she is behind the curve. Everyone is having fun but this person has a slight gasp. Nature hikes is an example where it becomes obvious who can handle a little bit of physical stress and who cannot. Games like volleyball, basketball, football, etc., are great as they require group participation and are opportunities for fun and realization of current conditions. The desire to change can come out of this.

5. Financial: The point is to show those who do not care at all that there are consequences to defying science. Many companies are adding to insurance cost premiums based on physical status and behavior. Many smokers pay more for insurance and we applaud this. Many policyholders can reduce their insurance cost via participation in positive health outcomes. Another way to say this is that those who do not participate get the opportunity to pay the highest premiums. The companies are trying to create positive behavior, and if you don't want to participate, then pay. Believe that you're worth the effort – honestly raise your self-esteem. Our prediction is that this approach will get more aggressive and ultimately create barriers to employment for the unhealthy.

I'll finish this section with a quote from the Dali Lama:

"Man sacrifices health in order to make money. Then he sacrifices money to recuperate his health. And then he is so anxious about the future that he does not enjoy the present; the result being that he does not live in the present or the future; he lives as if he is never going to die, and then dies having never really lived."

Don't be this person. Use Arthur Ashe's comment to lead you: "Start where you are. Use what you have. Do what you can."

Young Kids

Nothing is more important than to help create, evolve, and develop a healthy self-esteem for our kids! The young are at the early stages of choosing and there are not many categories as important as being fit minded. At an early age, activate an awesome nutrition plan. Learn to eat as a family, learn to eat healthy, prepare food at home, and have your children involved in the preparation. They will love to help. At an early age, take these kids camping, to the park, hiking, OUTDOORS and away from the screens. The benefits of an active relationship between child and parent cannot be overstated. And guess what? You need to be involved in this too. The child must see you working as well. You can choose your own stuff but kids must see you trying. Their self-esteem will be healthy from the beginning, and this will serve them well throughout. I have a strong belief that the child who grows up valuing their health and fitness will garner more success than those who know how to push buttons on a screen.

If you have not done great with young kids, accept this as true and move on. These are your kids we're talking about and a serious effort at this juncture will pay off for the rest of your – and their – lives. What should you do?

Develop a plan that includes YOU. Monkey see, monkey do is real. Children need to see you trying. You do not have to succeed but your determination needs to be on full display. When you "fail" at something, be sure to laugh, get back up and try again. Understand that you are not the only one watching this situation. Little eyes see you and will accept your choices as to what is important. If you do not have an idea on what to do, get with your confidant and develop one. Choose something that excites you and you want to succeed at. The axiom that something is better than nothing, is crazy. YOU have to like the activity. Do not settle. Do not let a lot of grass grow. Get at this. Get started. Sooner is absolutely better than later.

With this in motion, become a confidant for your child. Ask compelling questions and listen. Your sincere interest in their desires is very important to their honesty. Your conversation with your confidant should have helped guide you to know what questions reveal the realities of your child and use that to guide them to an activity that is fun and enduring. Understand that temporary success is OK as it will lead to their next activity. All OK!

Now find and provide the best venue to activate that activity and get out of the way.

Kids

If you have done great with the young kids, you're in the evolvement stage – keep up the good work and get them involved in activities that they enjoy. Usually team sports become available. T-ball and the like. These are good, but let the child choose. For evolving, I'm partial to anything that allows for individual development, such as rock climbing, trampolines, riding a bicycle, etc. Each of these require a singular development and self-esteem is only boosted when this exact person succeeds at a task. Encourage this behavior and you'll have a self-reliant child going forward. A watch-out would be to NOT be a "helicopter" parent. Your child will get bumps and bruises, fail often, and just plain suck at some things. If they've selected an activity and are struggling, then teach them more how to get back on the pony and ride. Success is way sweeter after a struggle. Celebrate with them and encourage them. That is enough.

Now find and provide the best venue to activate that activity and get out of the way. This is theirs! Assistance is to mean that you make sure they have the best equipment you can afford. Understand that less than perfect has benefits as the child will learn to overcome difficulties and their self-esteem will be the better for it.

Believe this though: Your children want to be the best. Help them.

Teenagers

If you've done a great job with your kids, continue the evolvement. Accept that your job is in maintenance mode and enjoy. You're not off the hook by any means as this age is rife with temptations that will veer your child into venues where you know disaster lurks. Your relationship with your child is probably open and honest, and you should leverage this to keep the kid on track. Discuss the pros and cons of the obvious temptations. One that I use for my children is the discussion at college orientations. Our speaker said to incoming students to look to the left of us and then to the right – two of the three of you will not be here in 4 years. Let that soak in a little bit. This means that sixty-six percent of college freshman will not complete their degree without a serious disruption. I tell my kids that I do not know what derailed this group but that they are derailed. When a temptation comes, and they will, try to get them to look at it through the long lens of life. Will this help take you where you want to go or is this a higher risk of derailing you? Choose wisely.

Understand that you will never get away from being a role model. You will have to keep up your endeavors as well. By the way, this is for your benefit too. Do your best to keep your child on track so they can have the best life possible.

If teenagers are not active, you are still their parent and obligated to their success. This is the point where your confidant is the MOST important. The solution for this situation has to be one hundred percent inclusive. You are assuredly part of the answer. You have to have your ducks in a row or be seriously moving in that direction. Your behavior and changes have to be obvious and most of all, sincere.

If your teenager is at a starting point, make sure that you sit with them and ask prompting questions and listen. This group will need to select an activity that incorporates convenience, fun, independence, and results. I would again recommend individual activities so that the child can believe in themselves. Understand that this person's self-esteem may not be the best. A gentle turn is needed to bend the curve. This kid is growing up and wants independence a lot. Your guidance has to be respectful of their current goals. Nutrition is more in this group's hands than in yours. What you keep around your house though is YOUR choice. If they want to eat crap, make them get it. Do not be an enabler, but do walk the fine line to keep doors open. Understand that "this is not happening" is OK, but pick your battles. You are not their friend. You are their parent. You cannot fix yesterday, but you can and should create a better tomorrow. As always, now is the time.

Conclusion

It is hard to understate the value of self-esteem. One hundred percent of us are affected by the philosophy that we subscribe to. All viewpoints on this subject lead to action by you. Our hope on the subject is to help you to identify yourself and add to your strengths and to minimize your weaknesses.

Those with a healthy self-esteem are choosing to integrate health, fitness, and general well-being throughout their lives. Challenges do exist and have their effect, but overall, nothing will stop this group from trying. Failure is inevitable but dismissed as part of life and the choice is to learn from it and move on. Vanity is not an issue as this group knows that what will be, will be and are OK with that. They will do their best and so be it.

Those with a façade-based self-esteem will struggle and be swayed by commentary from others, and failure is disturbing to them. This group does not like to fail but do so as a result. Our goal is to get this group to realize that they are in their own way. Choosing to step outside of themselves and to go for results-based fitness goals will lead them to a healthier lifestyle and they will then achieve the best "looks" they can achieve. We all need to be happy with our best.

Those with a do-not-care-at-all approach are a difficult group and our goal is to get this group to realize that their future is worth valuing and also in their hands alone. Various factors should drive this group to rethink their future and through various means "come to the table" and see what they're missing. Those who are more fit and fit-minded need to help and encourage this group as much as possible. All will win if all are involved.

For kids, self-esteem could not be more important. At any stage of their life, they are your kids and you have an opportunity to positively affect their self-esteem. While this responsibility is daunting sometimes, do not forget that your confidant is there to help you. You need a sincere source of logic to help you and you should use them. Even if things are going well, use them for advice on the next step. You and your kids are worth it.

One aspect to notice on this chapter is that we did not open up the idea regarding significant others. This was not an accident as the first word on self-esteem is to be taken seriously. You are you and your actions will influence others. Waiting on others to take this step with you usually serves to provide an excuse for inaction. You drive your ship. It's as simple as that.

Chapter Five
Economics

Building a personal and solid economic base is crucial to our well-being and peace of mind. We all want to have the financial acumen to choose to do as we please, when we want to. If your health and fitness are in good shape, then the likelihood that your financial situation is solid is much higher. In other words, you can have your financial security if you work for it (and not necessarily need a high income to achieve this).

To me, this is where the rubber hits the road as being healthy and fit means so much more than just money. If you are healthy and fit, you are most likely able to stay out of the hospital, doctor's office, pharmacy, etc., and understand that many tangible benefits come from it. You have the time – and probably the money – to enjoy the opportunities available to you. Active adventures appeal to you. You are not satisfied with simply "being there" and watching.

Fitness is the best investment that you will ever make. The actual money that you spend to become healthy and fit comes back to you many times over. Be choosy as you spend money. Spending money should incorporate a comprehensive approach so that we do not undermine our own values.

We are inundated with marketing schemes that are determined to get our money and provide only momentary satisfaction for it. We are told, repetitively, that we deserve whatever is being sold. Cars, food, entertainment, technology, etc. It's like we keep searching for a new "high," and won't be satisfied until we find it. What we may discover, if we step back, is that this satisfaction doesn't exist and never has. While we all enjoy a brief escape from life, we have to come back. While we spent money on these frivolities, we probably let them take our focus away from our health. We lose ground in the process.

Spending money should purchase results that help the whole us. Momentary benefits are OK, but should not take precedence over the larger picture. We cannot deny the following: By far, the largest cause of bankruptcy in America is due to health-related issues. What this means is that your health and fitness are directly tied to your financial well-being. We spend a large amount of time working on our top-end earnings. We all like to get raises and talk about how much we make. My response has always been that it doesn't matter how much you make as much as it matters how much you keep. Being healthy and fit means that you will spend less on medical care.

Nothing, and I mean nothing, is lower cost than not getting sick. This next comment will be considered mean: Getting sick is mostly a choice.

According to a 2016 report[1] from the Centers for Medicare & Medicaid Services, the people of the United States spend over three trillion dollars per year on healthcare (which really should be called sick care). This does not include research either. Three trillion dollars goes from one pocket (yours) and into another. This breaks down to $10,348 for every man, woman, and child in the US today. This spending can and should be mostly prevented. This is 17.9% of the US economy. Anyone see a problem?

When we choose to exercise, eat right, get enough sleep, not smoke, etc., then we are also choosing to avoid a disease that could require major medical intervention. We, collectively, could avoid most of the three trillion dollars' worth of care.

With some rare exceptions, type 2 diabetes is a choice. And that means that ALL of the collateral damage from this type of diabetes becomes a choice as well. Other illnesses such heart disease, cancer, and arthritis each have a common thread of poor lifestyle choices.

Choose to be healthy. The odds of your success are in your hands.

So what does it cost to be healthy?

For basic, high quality health, the actual answer is little to nothing. What is needed is good food, water, sleep, and exercise. Be efficient in getting healthy. Get results effectively! And the sooner the better!

---

[1] https://www.cms.gov/Research-Statistics-Data-and-Systems/Statistics-Trends-and-Reports/NationalHealthExpendData/Downloads/NHE-Presentation-Slides.pdf

For the moderately to highly motivated, the following is a guide:

A reasonable gym membership = $40/month

Workout apparel = $10/month

Gym shoes = $10/month

Gym snacks (bars, gels, nuts) = $25/month

This comes out to about $3.00 per day. The current cost of being sick = $25.21/day.

If you need or want coaching, add $120 per month.

We are humans. We need to be maintained. We understand maintenance. We are completely accustomed to the idea that we need to maintain our car by changing the oil. We know that we're to have our teeth cleaned. We even know that we need to do the dishes to avoid buying new ones. What is cool about these three examples is that we know them well enough to actually do them. We do them because it's the right thing to do, and that through this minimal preventive maintenance we know that we are saving big bucks on repair and avoiding buying new things. It always fascinates me to watch people skimp out on maintenance and then make a big project about a repair that could have been avoided. A thirty-dollar oil change can prevent a two-thousand-dollar engine repair. Basically, change your oil and don't buy junk gas. Why would you not?

Traditionally, the cost of an emergency repair is ten times the cost of preventative maintenance. This is what I'm asking you to do. Take care of your health while it's still cheap. Why don't we?

While the money paid for our body repairs may be borne by our employer through Medicare, insurance, etc., the true cost of the repair is borne by the patient. This person is the one that had or has a lingering illness or catastrophic event, and needs unplanned downtime to repair and recuperate. Surgery may be required, and this person will be off work, may lose their job, become disabled or all other sorts of negative consequences. Divorce and bankruptcy frequently happen due to these illnesses and (I'm on my soapbox again) could have been prevented. Do not let a penny get in the way of a dollar. Take care of your health while it's still cheap. Three dollars/day planned is much better than twenty-five dollars/day unexpected.

The economic and emotional impact of an illness cannot be understated. Many times, when these bad things happen, the news generally gets worse and worse, and the end of these negative consequences never seems to come. Take care of your health while it's still cheap.

We should do all that we can to take good of care of our bodies as we do our car or even our cell phone. When we maintain our bodies through proper nutrition and physical exercise, we are saving big bucks (along with many other tangible benefits). We all know this, and it only takes about a half hour/day with proper planning. Use your confidant to help you make this process efficient so that you can still enjoy the other 164.5 hours/week. Remember: YOU Matter!

I do believe that I am preaching to the choir about taking care of yourself. You will be healthier, live longer, not have illnesses and all the negative consequences that come with them. I know that you know this.

What stops us then? In this chapter, we're discussing economics so I will deal with that issue and let the other "reasons" be discussed in other chapters.

One of the primary reasons is that in America today, the cost of preventative healthcare is borne by the recipient and this expense prevents people from affording it. If I just ask you to ignore this as an issue, I am sure that a lot of you will just ignore me. If this paragraph is speaking to you, please look at taking care of yourself as an investment. Remember that three dollars per day spent now avoids twenty-five dollars/day (plus the associated grief that goes with it.)

And just like all the other important things in our life: Time is of the essence. There are economic reasons to getting healthy efficiently. A lot of horrible information exists that can and will take you down the wrong road, and you may not realize this for a long time, causing you to lose faith in being healthy on your own and become a person who makes frequent and unnecessary trips to your doctor.

This is a serious issue because the real goal of this bad information is to get you to buy their crap. And if wasting money on these paths is awful, it's not near as awful as the point that your time has been wasted. You could have been healthy a long time ago if you had not listened to the noise and this is time that you will never get back!

Being efficient means that you learn and understand the right path to take towards being healthy. I cannot emphasize enough the role of your confidant. You need to sit down with your confidant and lay out an effective plan that includes estimating which resources you will need. The importance of a competent confidant is not to be dismissed. This person has to have YOUR health in mind. They have to understand that health is not just the absence of sickness but reflects the physical and mental ability to do what's important to YOU.

Money seems to always be an issue, so I want explain a very important point that we will all recognize and accept in theory, but fuss about in practice. So, here it is: "Do not let a penny get in the way of a dollar."

Please understand that there are higher costs associated with your health not being where you want and need it to be. According to the American Diabetes Association, in 2017, the average health care costs for people with diabetes was over $16,000 per year[2]. Being overweight is expensive. It results in additional medical expenditures, lost work, and higher insurance premiums. I am not suggesting that you spend as much as possible at all. The resources you choose need to help you achieve being healthy and to reach your goals.

As a fitness center owner, I cannot tell you the number of times that we answer the phone to hear the price question. What I want to scream into the phone is: "What does it matter?"

"Will my fitness center make you healthy or not?"

"Come in and look around. We will gladly sit down with you and explain our philosophy and show you our center so that you can make an informed decision regarding how we fit with your goals. I promise that you will get your prized question answered but I'm imploring you to make your investigation thorough."

---

[2] https://www.diabetes.org/resources/statistics/cost-diabetes

There is always a fear that if you commit to a gym that you cannot get out of it – that you will not follow through on your plan – and then "Look at all of the wasted money!"

Let's go about this issue from a different perspective. The commitment that you are making is to yourself and your family. There aren't enough excuses on the planet to justify not giving it your best effort. No doubt that there are things that happen, but the ones that cannot be worked around are rare. Most of the issues relate to complacency and boredom. My suggestion for everyone is to that you take your fitness effort to the highest level. Get rowdy and make a big deal of your goals! What this may mean is for you to commit to an event that you have always wanted to do but did not believe that you were capable of. Make this event a travelling vacation to a place that you want to go; a 5K in another state, a bike ride on the other side of the country. Plan to take your family to a theme park somewhere so they can go with you while you do your thing. Then, blast the news on social media. Basically, commit, commit, and then commit again! Dream big.

What this dream does is "forces" you to act on your commitment. When you have to do that 5K, that bike ride, whatever you planned, you have to be ready by the time the date comes. You have effectively boxed yourself into behaving. Others are counting on you, and you have to perform. Awesome! You cannot back out so you may as well succeed at the event.

Guess what happens when you do this? YOU succeed and are truly on your way to a healthier you. Have as much fun as you can!

Am I saying that all spend on fitness is valid? Nope!

I will not understand the concept of treating bogus information as factual if it comes from an authentic sounding entity. I am sure that you hear about enough "promising" solutions to your wellness that sound too good to be true. The shakes, gadgets, widgets, cardio equipment, books, etc., are amazing in their success. They are frequently purchased by a consumer who, if asked, knows the purchase will not work. Why? The only answer that comes to me is that the seller has worked very hard making themselves "credible." They hire spokespeople who are willing to state that their "amazing" success was only due to the item being sold and that this opportunity is available for you as well – for money. These companies know that if they hire a person with a PhD, a segment of the consumer base will consider this enough information and make the buy. This approach happens down the line, product by product, book by book, plan by plan. Perhaps the consumer feels overwhelmed and that by making this attempt, they can say to their friends and relatives that they are at least trying. Basically, this group is buying the item and then creating the goal. I am calling bullshit.

If a consumer knows that the item they are going to purchase will not work, DO NOT BUY IT! This is not a zero-sum game. You are not just risking the money you are going to spend because by buying the bogus item you are obligated to at least try it. You will not realize that you will fail immediately – and when you do – you will blame yourself. You have done something wrong or the gadget, book or plan would have surely worked. The only thing you did wrong was to buy the thing and waste precious time determining that it will not work. Now it may take months or years before you put your toe back in the water to try the next costly idea. Chances are that the same exact purchasing process will be repeated and will achieve the same exact result. And now we are on to round three (maybe) and probably several years have gone by. You are now in the worst shape of your life and life is getting much more complicated. You cannot see a way out.

Here is a truism: Goals are not obvious and the devil is in the detail. Losing weight seems to be everyone's go-to goal and this is sort of fine. Another common goal is to return to your glory days. Both of these goals are considered generic. The goals that you are after need to be specific. The issue becomes how and why. When generic goals are settled on and the "why" is not developed, then shortcuts seem to become logical answers. Price is important when shortcuts come into play because you don't believe in any of this anyway. This group seeks the easy and cheap way out. They seek a cheap gym membership and then want to diet and supplement their way towards their goal. They'll spend a fortune on that crap. This approach is the most common, and I have never seen it work – short-term nor long-term. Another side effect of this failing approach is nothing will be learned. These mistakes will either be repeated or the goal given up on and genetics will, somehow, be blamed.

A good goal will be measurable and reachable – specific. Data across several functions needs to be collected prior to starting your journey. This practice forces you to create comprehensive goals. Get a qualified trainer to develop a data collecting process for you and see where you stand. A single point goal (think weight) will not qualify as a goal and you need to go back to work to create a comprehensive one.

If weight loss (generic) is your initial thought, then convert this to: I would like to lower my A1C to less than six, achieve blood pressure within the normal range, a resting heart rate below 70, etc. I would also like to get ten percent stronger across all domains and be able to cover a mile is less than eight minutes. If you achieve these converted goals, I promise you that your weight will lower and you will feel and be better. There is no sense in focusing on a single point, as something else will get out of whack in the process. Focus on several and watch them all improve!

If returning to your glory days (generic) is your goal, then convert it this to: I would like to set up a strength matrix and then get on an improvement plan that incorporates stamina and strength so that I can watch the numbers climb over time. My bet is that your health will drastically improve and you won't even realize it.

Never forget this truism: The closest distance between two points is a straight line.

This is how goals should be set: You and your confidant need to sit down and determine the real goals for you and then determine the straightest path to achieve these goals. You are right. Money will need to be spent to achieve them. This is the time to make a buying decision. What do you need to achieve your goals? Fill in the blanks defining what you need and then find the correct services to fulfil them. These services may be free or they may cost. If they do cost (and they probably will) and you do not feel that you can afford them, then please look at your current spending. There is a high chance that you can find more than enough and that you will come out way ahead as well. Do not forget that: Nothing, and I mean nothing, is lower cost than not getting sick.

The economic approach to looking at life should not be viewed as selfish or condescending. This approach is valuable as it helps define what is valuable to you. We hear from religious leaders that the government budget is a moral document, and I agree with that in your personal life as well. Take an hour to sit back and write down the ways that you spend money that doesn't lead to true happiness and assign its true cost. Here are some of mine: TV = $160/month. While I love watching shows on my DVR, I recognize that this is too much. Is this in the way of my health and fitness goals? Sweets = $30/month. I do like sugar, but $30/month? Am I kidding myself? I need to cut this in half. I am not happier for eating them and causing myself harm by doing so. Coffee = $15/month. I have a pot in my office and at home. I make this easy. I also actually like mine better. I'm not happier because I buy coffee by the cup.

The three examples above amount to $205/month or $2,460/year in after tax money which means that I had to gross $3,514 to buy this crap that really only marginally helped my happiness.

With this $2,460/year, I could buy a trainer, a new bike (and this will last more than a year), new shoes, a fitness event, travel to an exciting destination, etc. Why would I not?

This is just me – other obvious categories are cell phones, fast food, cigarettes, alcohol, car payments, clothes, credit cards, etc. We each have areas that can be tapped for better service.

Some of the answer is that peer pressure allows me to buy stuff that doesn't matter but scoffs at purchases that will actually help me. Tell someone that you are going on a cruise and watch their eyes light up and offer their hearty congratulations to the lucky you. Then tell that same person that you are investing in yourself and getting a personal trainer to help you get healthy and watch them ask: Why? You can do that yourself. My basic question is if we could do that (as if fitness is a *that*) ourselves, then why don't we?

Another answer is that we do not believe in ourselves and that we will work to achieve the goals set. If this is your fear, then revisit your goal to make sure that all components of that goal are what you really want. If the answer is wobbly, then recognize that and do not be hard headed. Change the goal to be realistic and take a moment to discover why the previous one was not right. Do not let the problem go unsolved – fix it.

After this simple (but important) exercise, make sure that you have identified a comprehensive list of resources needed to succeed and develop a way to get these. Be very picky on these items. Often folks purchase way too much of the wrong thing for the appearance of being fashionable or presumed serious. I'm firmly on the page of minimalism. If the item doesn't absolutely help my journey, then the thing should not have been applied to this journey or maybe even bought.

Take an honest look at the rest of your expenditures to see if you believe them to represent who you want to be. Your past three months bank statement and credit card(s) are great places for accurate relatable information.

What you spend money on equals the definition of a priority. What you spend the most on represents your highest priority. Usually housing, auto, food make it into the top three and this is probably correct. Move down the list to make sure that you mean what you are actually doing. Anything catch your eye? Are your priorities where they need to be? While you are in the midst of evaluating your life, now is also the time to identify all areas of improvement. You do not have to make any crazy adjustments – but if you see something glaring – feel free to fix it. After your adjustment, evaluate the difference. Is this what you wanted it to be? Yes – move on. No – change again.

One area that I want to come back to as it relates to economics, is the influence that we allow outsiders to have. We are subjected to intrusive commentary from friends and family (some of whom we rarely ever see) who examine our plate at holidays, parties, outings, etc. And they hurt. We are trying to make positive changes in our lives and those we love and respect the most are right there with their stabbing words belittling our efforts. Why? I'll never know. The best advice that I have is to ignore them. My belief is that the more we ignore these comments, the less likely we are to continue to receive them. On the other hand, if we cave to these comments, the more we will receive them and the harder our goal just became. To unravel your efforts and plans will only harm you and the end result. Time will have gone by and if you do restart (and I hope you do), the costs will be amazingly higher (but way less than if you do not restart). This is a difficult to work through but you will become more skillful at thwarting the attacks the more you challenge them.

Life does get in the way. What if I do have to restart?

1. I am sorry.
2. Evaluate what happened and see if you could have done something differently. Many times, you cannot and I will not preach to you. You make the best choices that you can and sometimes, something has to give. Usually it's you, and I am sorry.
3. Go back to the beginning of this chapter and try it again. Giving up is not an option.

You may feel selfish, but do not. Your good health is what can help you cope with whatever happened and will help you find the best solution to your issue. And you will get healthier as a result. Sucks that you lost some time but you did what you had to do and now you are back and probably smarter than before. I'm OK with that.

For kids:

Economics is a challenge for kids, but this also is an area that needs explored from a pragmatic point-of-view. I acknowledge that we all want to be the best parents that we can be and that we know that we are being judged by others and that we judge ourselves. I'm sure that our kids are judging us and we send them very confusing signals when we become wishy-washy. Spend some time and explore and evaluate your belief system and then stick to it. You are fine and not fine at the same time. Do your best and don't worry about it.

Understand that you are being watched. From when they are little to when they are young adults. You are being watched by your children. This is actually good in that you know that you are being held accountable. If you run their expectations through your head when you make an effort or a purchase, then you will make a better choice.

A great way to look at purchases for your kids is through the eyes of an investor. You don't want to drive yourself nuts thinking about every little thing but understand that they do add up to a message. Is the message one that you want to send?

Make sure that most of your purchases correlate to your belief system. If your kid needs a new pair of shoes: Are the pair that you're buying of a quality that will allow their safe participation in their chosen activity? I've seen people make this mistake, and I want you to avoid it. I will use shoes as an example but understand that this logic translates throughout purchases.

The child will want to begin an activity and the parent will not be sure if they are serious or not and they do not want to lose money. So, they go the cheap route to get shoes. This way, the logic states, they won't be out much if the activity doesn't work out. The issue with this logic (for you or your child) is the poor choice of shoes will influence – negatively – the result of the activity chosen. What will be left unknown – maybe for life – is if the child walks away from the activity; was it due to not liking the activity or was it the cheap shoes? For you as the parent, if the activity was deemed to be a good one, put some serious thought into it – yes or no. If yes, then invest in quality wear. Please understand that I'm not asking you to spend a lot of money on shoes. I am asking that you purchase the right ones though. Then you can be more confident with your child's result.

Your goal as a parent is to instill a healthy lifestyle in your child with the knowledge that you are choosing an ultimate low-cost lifestyle for them. A few dollars here or there may lead to your kid's life free of diabetes, cancer, heart disease, joblessness, bankruptcy, etc. The legacy that you are creating for your child begins at birth and really never ends until you do.

Conclusion

Being unhealthy is a choice that has enormous costs associated with this. I am begging you to choose to be healthy for your sake, your family's sake, for economic reasons, for quality of life reasons. Basically: Choose that YOU MATTER. Understand that no one needs to be type 2 diabetic. Obesity is not a genetic matter. I know that not all of us (actually very, very few of us) will be amazing athletes and the world will be in awe of us. I get it. That, though, is not the choice. Choose to be healthy. It's more than worth it.

I have laid out a plan with reasoning to efficiently become physically healthy. Your confidant is your key to success. Choose this person wisely and use them effectively. Believe in yourself. Your life does indeed rely on this. Making good choices throughout your life will pay you back handsomely. Some of the choices will be difficult to make, but make them anyway. When you choose to not make good choices, accept that you did so and come back as soon as you can. You will be glad you did.

Understand that it is OK to invest money to accomplish your goals. Look at it through the lens of investment and understand that just spending the money doesn't necessitate the ROI (return on investment). In this case, as in most, you have to work the money. Focus on getting healthier and then count the returns. Do not fool yourself into believing that this would have happened anyway. It probably would not have.

Your effort gave you the return on investment – nothing else.

Your kids are your legacy. What you model to them will be enacted by them. Consider your purchases an investment so that you look at them correctly. Not all purchases fall into this category, but the ones that do need the honest evaluation. Make your kids successful with healthy living and this effort will pay you back handsomely too. Imagine your life if your family practiced healthy living. Pretty awesome, isn't it?!

Chapter Six
Quality of Life

A high quality of life is not overrated (and not that hard to have either).

A high quality of life is not overrated – should not have to be said at all – ever. Having a high quality of life should be an obvious goal for everyone. We all know this but the willingness to live it is not something we do well as a society. What is high quality of life? Why not? What is in our way? How do we know? What do we have to do?

I'll start with "What is high quality of life?" This can be one of the most important questions of the whole book as it pertains to "Why am I doing this?" A high quality of life is simple as it really means to be truly satisfied with yourself. Break this concept down to the next step: "What is truly satisfied?" To be truly satisfied, you need to look at "what is real" versus "what is told to you is real." They're different. What is real is you, your family, your health, and your values. These four concepts will encompass the vast majority of your satisfaction. What is not real, yet we very much value, involves money, looks, jobs, pleasure…things – you know – vanity. This kind of stuff always seems to take priority in our lives and a lot of the reasoning is that we temporarily make others "happy" when we cater to these things. Understand that in the world of "what is told to you is real" VERY frequently involves the need to buy something and this purchase makes others temporarily happy. Doing this perpetuates the problem to others as well (Here's a secret: They aren't happy either.) When we peel our own onion and put our discoveries in these two piles, we can see them more honestly. And as we are more honest, we can better see where our priorities lie. To be truly satisfied is a very worthwhile goal. This is involved but it's not selfish.

In the world of fitness, to be truly satisfied, we should value enhanced capabilities to their highest end. Our ability to be more physically productive leads to a higher satisfaction as more rely on us and choose us to complete a task they need completed. Those who are more fit are more reliable and capable. They're the "go-to" crowd to get honest advice and direction. They're the ones who no one doubts can accomplish what they strive to do and they're also the ones who are being watched for their next activity with wonderment. An improvement in lean muscle mass will lead to an improvement in stamina, strength, and agility and will serve us well into our old age. An awesome win for us! This is how the world of fitness should be.

In reality, the world of fitness mostly comprises of the need to constantly answer the question: "How much weight did you lose?" I understand how we got to believing the only purpose of fitness is to lose weight but am sincerely hoping to alter its value to nothing. The internet, media, medical community, and marketing constantly assail us with the need to lose weight. A more correct way to state the need is to say that we need to improve the composition of our weight by reducing fat and increasing lean muscle mass. This is too much of a mouthful so we stick with "lose weight" and then build a huge empire of marketing to achieve just that. Many gyms cater to weight loss, practically the whole New Year's resolution fiasco is built around weight loss. We have weight loss surgery. Weight loss pills populate shelves everywhere. Diet books are always popular. Yet obesity is rampant and depression is going through the roof. Maybe another approach is more effective? We sincerely want the right thing but there is more money to be made in telling you that you want weight loss only so that is what you are told. The results of this weight loss mindedness? Crap. Quality of life with this approach? Crap. Instead of going or continuing to go down this road, we need to actually do the right thing. Eat right. Exercise correctly. Sleep right. Minimize stress, and really watch the magic happen. I'm challenging you to do this for six sincere months. You'll be amazed! You will experience a higher quality of life by becoming stronger, healthier, and more energetic. Go for it!

A serious problem is just simply believing that a high quality of life can be achieved through living right. The concept that this is too much work with too little payoff or it takes too long to achieve will prevent well-meaning, able-bodied people from participating in behavior that will enhance their lives. Basically, if you don't begin, you won't get the benefits. Begin! Take the easiest steps that offer the highest and quickest payback. Sleep eight hours. Drink plenty of water. Eat non-processed foods. These are easy. They only require small changes to your lifestyle and offer big benefits. You'll notice results right away through lower stress and increased health. You now have a reason to believe that "Hey, you're on the right track!" What a moment! Now expand into the rest of the living right mantra. Add exercise, invest in activities that excite you, create a Good Food Items (Chapter 8), push yourself to be your best and watch your quality of life rise exponentially. You're worth it. Why wouldn't you?

Another existing problem is that we are wired to value others before ourselves. We believe that we are selfish if we focus on ourselves first. I would argue that unless we focus on ourselves first, we can never be truly not selfish. You, your family, your health, and your values – all together – create an infrastructure for you to be free to appropriately help others. If all these values are honestly satisfied, then it's easy and OK to reach out to other's needs, and you will do a great job of it. Giving up on any of these four will make you try to balance non-critical needs with those that really matter to you. You'll struggle, and no one will win. High quality self-satisfaction is a true launch pad to assisting others effectively and, therefore, it is not selfish at all.

To efficiently get yourself to where you are truly satisfied means that your prioritization is effective. Exercise, sleep, and proper nutrition are essential to a high-energy go-getter who can influence family and friends to do the same. Be sincere and understand that exercising your values means that other's opinions are to be considered, but you have the final say. And you need to be OK with that. Many will try to entice you with trivial satisfiers – usually food or drink – and try to divert you from what is important to you. You need to be more than OK with telling them no.

This leads to the question that I wish wasn't necessary. Why do we not strive for a high quality of life? Why would we do that? Not striving for a high quality of life surely isn't a thing is it? Well, yeah, it kinda is.

One of the primary reasons for our acceptance of a poorer quality of life than we should have is our feeling that others deserve it more than we do. We're sure that if we focus on our happiness that others will suffer. This is not a zero-sum game. If we are not truly happy, it's very likely that we'll drag others down with us and we'll all wallow in misery. The better answer is to get up and make the most of your day. Each day counts and should include time to either nurture an interest or to further concrete plans to bring something that you enjoy alive. I like obstacle course racing and long organized bike rides. Each day for me includes time working out and/or planning to succeed at some future event. I am aware that for me to succeed in my ventures, I need to consider nutrition, exercise, logistics, equipment, rest, peaking with fitness, etc. Each of these subjects are enjoyable to me, and I like to learn about them. This "stuff" is a part of who I am, and I like it. I believe that my focus on these subjects allows me to not worry about the small stuff and that allows me to be a better person as I'm not into anyone else's business. I appreciate everyone's approach to life and hope that I inspire others to value and to go for their dreams as well. An attitude of "To each their own." suits me. I don't have any jealousy towards what others do and am glad they are doing it. I've got my own thing, and if others want to participate – great. If they don't – great. As long as they're participating in something, I'm happy for them. How can I help?

Another reason for accepting a lower quality of life: Hesitation. I've seen many people speak grandiosely about plans they have, and I'm excited for them. When I check up with them later, I discover that the plan has been derailed by blah, blah, blah. These folks have made serious strides of showing their sincerity of achieving a goal and then something got in the way preventing a great outcome from occurring, and I feel bad for their situation. This is a fine line for people as real obstacles do occur (just not all the time for every plan.) The reality is that this is their situation and not mine. What to do about this? If you're the doer, keep doing. If you see yourself as an excuse machine, look honestly at your planning and maybe don't pick something so big. The satisfaction you will receive from a smaller goal will be less, but the hope is that it'll whet your appetite to grab a higher goal and/or keep pursuing the smaller ones and be happy there. In any way that you look at it, it is better to do – than to say you will – and then don't. Develop a goal and accomplish it. If you are struggling to define a goal, please get with your confidant or close friend and develop one. A high quality of life should not be viewed as optional, but please understand that one is not guaranteed for you either. You need to develop the realities and make them happen. You, and others, will be glad that you did.

Illness and injury create a feeling of hopelessness and definitely lowers the quality of life. Some of the illnesses are not preventable due to genetics and some accidents just happen. You're hurt, and you are down. These sucks and we get through them the best that we can. A temporary period of a lower quality of life may occur and motivation may take a hit, but you can and should bounce back. These incidences probably are the best opportunities to visit and discuss your situation with a confidant. Thinking clearly is hard at this time, and you need help. We get X amount of time to enjoy life and you are never going to be younger than you are right this second. Do your best to get back on track to enjoy life and don't hesitate to ask for help. You are too important to watch several years go by before seizing an opportunity to live. Get on it now.

A persistent cause of a lower quality of life for people is a "cheapskate" attitude. The idea that if you don't spend money on things or events that you'll have enough to cover "necessities." I do not want to trivialize situations but do want to encourage you to evaluate your approach to life. It is easy to say no to events as they "cost too much." Some do. Some don't. Do the ones that don't, and explore your enjoyment of them. Love it? Keep doing it! Not sure? Find something else – but find it!

A large point of this book is to coach and teach you that through diligent preparation, you can prevent disease and injury. I encourage you to prepare for success. Competent confidants are great sources of planning and can work with you to ensure you have a lower cost of living and a higher quality of life. Use them.

I watched a video recently asking a question to those in their later years regarding, "What do you regret about your life?" The overwhelming answer wasn't what they did in life but what they didn't do. The chances they didn't take, the opportunities they passed on, the love they didn't seek, and the trips they didn't go on were a large source of regret for them. My quest for you is to do all you can to put yourself in a position to live a full life. I want you to experience the opportunities that come your way, to go where you want to, to do what you want when you get there. I basically want you in a position to get off the couch and live. You will be glad that you did!

The quality of life for our children is of paramount importance as their self-esteem is established early in life. If they are not active nor have a passion to pursue, there is a reasonable chance that their self-esteem will suffer. An interesting occurrence for me is discovering how kids talk about their parents to other kids. What do YOU want them to say? I want my children to say that their dad jumped at any chance to have fun and try new things. By giving my kid's something to talk to others about, I sense pride in their conversations with friends. Please understand that I'm doing "right living" for me, but I know that others (ones very important to me) are watching and reporting. This gives me motivation as well.

Chapter Seven
Fail

Why are we failing?

In 2017, the United States had over 36 thousand gyms with over 56 million members in them. There are diet plans, diet books, diet foods, gurus galore, etc., and yet we are one of the fattest, most unhealthy populations on the planet. Why?

Why – after spending scads more on "healthcare" than anywhere in the world – are we so amazingly bad at it? To say that Americans are not interested in their health isn't true. We are! What are we doing so wrong?

Let's simplify this so that we don't overwhelm ourselves with the problem or the solution. Basically, we've insisted that being healthy be complicated. There is more crap out there regarding information, devices, plans, etc. than we can shake a stick at. If we peel the onion back enough, we'll discover that the reasoning for the gross complication is…money. What a lot of the health and fitness industry folks have discovered is that if you're confused – but want something – that you will keep buying stuff ad nauseum. If the "answer" given to you is complicated, you'll keep buying. From THEIR viewpoint –

awesome! The problem is reasonably easy. We're overweight, lazy, and only pretend to care. The solution is also reasonably easy. Eat right. Exercise. Sleep. Keep stress under control (naturally).

The funny part is that you can buy the solution for practically nothing. We need to eat, so we should eat right. Sleep is a given. Keep your stress under control and get enough sleep. Eight hours a night is a great target. Exercise is free if you have access. If not, get to a quality fitness center and stay the hell away from cheap gyms. Why is this hard? Seventy percent of the deaths in America are directly tied to chronic disease. But one of the usual copouts is: "I can't afford it." Really? You can afford open-heart surgery? A stroke? Type 2 diabetes? Bariatric surgery? Not to mention the lost time with your family due to a self-induced chronic illness and its associated suffering. Your health is an investment. This is true in either direction. If you invest, you get a solid return with dividends. If you don't invest, you get to pay and then pay the dividends too. This becomes your choice. No one can escape this predicament.

Let's say we spend $10,000 per year per person on healthcare. And that 75% of all healthcare spending in the US is focused on chronic diseases. This amounts to approximately $7,500 per year for every man, woman, and child in America – just to cover the cost of chronic diseases. Basically, your healthcare's total cost should not exceed $2,500 per year. Does it? Don't just do out of pocket. That number can be skewed. The total medical cost is the number that you're after. And let's say that approximately 20% ($1,500) of chronic disease costs are due to genetic issues. This means that $6,000 per year for every man, woman, and child in healthcare costs for Americans is due to chronic diseases that are preventable through healthy living. Lifestyle choices do matter!

Can't afford it? Sleep isn't expensive. Make food and eat at home. Good food might be priced a little more than cheap crap, but please tell me you find yourself worth it. Please. Exercise two and a half hours per week. Learn to manage stress. Done! If you can do these four things correctly, there is a good chance that you'll be healthy.

What's the next reason? "I don't have time" comes to mind.

My response is: You don't have time to be healthy? Really? Being healthy is cost effective, more fun, you feel better, you can get a lot more done and be better at doing it. What's not to like?

You're sort of right. Being healthy is a transition that takes commitment and time. I tell people that you can get 90% of what you want in six months of honest effort. You will have to sincerely mean it to be efficient at it. There are ways to accomplish this. Get a confidant to help you is the best answer that I know of. You'll also have detractors trying their best to bring you down. You'll have to choose how to deal with them so you don't go crazy. But deal with them. You are important and need to accept that.

Next: "I don't know what to do first." Answer: There are four points of focus. Nutrition, Exercise, Sleep, and Stress. Keep it simple and focus on these. The other stuff is just noise.

Nutrition: Eat real food (not supplements.)

Exercise: Commit to two-and-a-half hours per week of intensive effort.

Sleep: You need eight hours per night. Get rid of distractions and do it.

Stress: Keep it to a minimum (None of us can escape stress entirely but do your best.)

See, we won't tell you what you don't know. We'll tell you how to succeed at what you do know.

This is going to be an interesting chapter in that the idea of fail will take on two meanings – one good and one bad. The bad sort of failing is what we tend to be the best at. Living a life that accepts poor choices as "the best that I could do" is BS and needs to be corrected as soon as possible. This type of failing often feels good while doing it, and then the ramifications are dismissed as "the way that it is." The good sort of failing is caused by honest efforts to improve ourselves and include the drive to succeed regardless of problems or discomfort created. This type of failing seldom feels good while doing it but the benefits allow you to achieve goals that you considered unimaginable. Often this type of failing leads to comments from "well-meaning" people who wonder why you continue on as you do. (Continue. Please.)

Fail: The wrong way

What is true failure? What is the wrong way to fail? From my view, failure revolves around a myth that you do not matter and that your temporary satisfaction is what does matter. This concept leads to a self-destructing behavior that will startle you if it's pointed out. And pointing it out is considered impolite. You will not want to hear it but you may recognize it or correlate it to your own behavior. To accept that your life is passé and that your health's priorities are dismissible should concern you to the point of anger. The reality though is that is what a lot of people truly do and guess what? Bad things happen. This is true failure and a common behavioral trait throughout our culture. We disguise our bad approaches to life in various ways and assume that we can reign in the problems through quick, cheap solutions that are sold over the counter. Oops.

Examples of personal failing with your health (You won't like some of these):

Obesity.

Type 2 diabetes.

Smoking.

Soda (including regular, diet and sweet tea).

Lack of sufficient exercise.

Shortage of proper sleep.

Fast food.

I believe that you truly understand the types of failure I'm referring to. Please stop these. You know that these beliefs and habits are not good for you. I am just willing to call them what they are. Failures.

To give you some insight of what true failure looks like in practice, please consider these examples: You might think it is OK to smoke or find it OK for someone else to smoke. You know, it's their right. And put vaping and dipping or chewing in this category too. That crap is nonsense as well.

There is no way that smoking (vape/dip/chew) is OK. If you smoke (vape/dip/chew), accept that this is a fail and then freaking stop. And while you are not in charge of others, you do not need to accept others' smoking (vaping/dipping/chewing) either.

You might consider it OK to eat fast food; after all, others do it. Really? Doesn't your body deserve better than that? Remember this is a self-help book that you are reading. And you are into it somewhat; why in heaven's name would you consider poor food choices OK? Fail!

You might be type 2 diabetic and eat fast food and drink soda and use tobacco. Please tell me that you know this is a fail? Do something sincere about this! I'm going to say this again. Most illnesses are the result of life choices. And this will make you cringe: 100% of type 2 diabetes is due to choice. Obesity is a choice. Stop lying to yourself, and even if you are partially right in that your genetics played a role- so freaking what. YOU deserve better.

If you start an exercise program and decide it's too hard – but you were seeing the results that you were seeking – and then you stop. Really? Fail. Or another way – half-assing through a workout and calling it a sincere effort. You know better. Fail!

On and on and on. The list of real failures are too numerous to mention but my belief is that you know what behavior that I am referring to. Stop it and go a different direction. Please!

Fail: Excuses

A big category of failure lands on the shoulders of excuses. I put these as a negative fail as they are prevalent and powerful in our society. They come in many forms preventing sincere self-improvement from happening.

We have all heard these and, at one time or another, have said/felt them: I don't have any money. I'm too fat. I'm too skinny. I'm too old. I'm too young. I'm too busy. I have kids. I don't have a car. My car won't work. I'm happy the way I am. Being healthy costs too much. I don't want to get bulky. How do I get rid of my belly? How do I get rid of the fat underneath my arms? The folks at the gym talked to me. The folks at the gym didn't talk to me. They don't have classes. The classes cost too much. I just need an elliptical, blah, blah, blah. You get one life. Do you really want excuses to determine YOUR fate?

Another huge arena for failure revolves around the crowd who doesn't want to ask for honest help and feels they already have the information they need to succeed. I feel really bad for this group as they want the right things and are moving towards improving. Their problem is that they have listened to the marketing from all of the wild sources out there that promise, by sending money their way, to "guarantee" great successes. The reason that I feel bad about this group is that they will become frustrated with the whole self-improvement thing and give up. In a way, I cannot blame them, but the reality is that you get one life. If you are living an unhealthy lifestyle and are suffering the consequences from that lifestyle, then any delay towards correcting it is a significant loss to you.

Healthy living and diligent work are the answers for 100% of everyone. Today is always the right time to start!

Fail: The right way

Let's discuss this: My personal belief is that those reading this self-help book really would like to achieve a goal. I now ask you – What is your goal? Now I want to get mean. Is it big enough? Are you asking enough of yourself? Do you think that reaching this goal will be easy? Whatever your goal is – be it career, family, health, and fitness, monetary, etc. – if your goal is big enough then you will struggle to achieve it and mess up a bunch along the way. Right? I'm not telling you anything you don't know. The question is: How do we use these mistakes to get our goal achieved? Above all, your goal is to be sincere and of honest value to you.

As you get started on these goals, chances are that you will try this on your own and/or you might surf the internet looking for the magic answers and will likely find out that none of this worked or only partially works. And you know that as you pursue these powerful goals – that "well-intentioned" people will advise you to calm down, give up, encourage you to accept that it's alright, you tried, etc. This verbiage makes success even harder as you are now being forced to push against this tide too. I am here to adjust your self-analysis to encourage you to keep going and consider the long-term benefits of your goals.

One of the usual approaches to people who seek a better life is to accuse them of thinking that they are better than everyone else. I've seen people try their hardest to achieve a goal and not make it. The people around them fall into either of two camps: Either 1. That's OK, you tried; or 2. See, you're no better than us. Failing is a common trait of success.

Wise failure (or even dumb failure) is a great pathway to success. As this book is a health and fitness improvement book, I'll focus there.

First, let's define failure in the manner that I'm talking about. This is pretty easy. In the positive context, failure means that you tried your best and didn't make it happen.

114

You aimed for an eight-minute mile but didn't achieve it. You ran nine-and-a-half minute miles. Is this a big deal? Not really. First tries seldom, if ever, work out. As you get better, your results will too!

So why do we struggle? Why is this a big deal? How did we get here?

One of the major issues that I see in the world of health and fitness is a strong desire by participants to believe themselves successful at life and all the components thereof.

As we begin life (post high school) and then move through our careers, we are astounded at the level of technical expertise that we can attain and just how proficient we get at tasks that we deemed over our heads just a few years ago. We often work to take our games to the next levels through education either at a technical school, online or actually at a university. The school of hard knocks is good too. We believe that this may take some time but that we can do this! We can have it all! Husband, wife, kids, house, vacation, vacation home, whatever! We can have it and we are willing to struggle to do it!

We develop a working knowledge of mathematics, computer science, chemistry, physics, etc. We can write twenty-page papers in an evening and score an A. We can weld. We can drive nails. Our jobs and careers become our persona. Nothing can get in our way.

Success comes, albeit difficult, but it comes and often that success comes at the costs of (here is where I chime in) our health. We skip out on sleep, exercise, eating properly, and think that we have discovered their lack of necessity. What is really important is to get ahead. We need to get to the highest level that we can achieve in the shortest time possible. We want the house, car, spouse, etc., that we deserve. We are fatigued at another challenge. That healthy living thing isn't really that hard compared to all that we just went through. Is it?

And the correct answer is…It wasn't, but now it is. The years taken to arrive at your current state of health can take a heavy toll. I am currently fifty-seven years old. Out of my high school class of approximately 300, approximately 10% of them are already passed for one reason or another. Most of these losses have come about via lifestyle choices that went bad. Please remember – success at the costs of your health is loss. What we all need to understand is that everyone needs to be serious. I view your health as a worthwhile challenge and YOU are the one in charge. My take is for a dedicated person to 90% retrieve their health requires them to be serious for six months. Serious is the key word here. I have stated the six-month concept in other chapters and would like to better define it here.

What is the definition of serious? What are the characteristics? This person plans for success and, out of the gate, develops a confidant to help them stick to a plan. This person carves out forty-five minutes to an hour for five of the seven days/week and then sticks to this for the full six months. This person comprehends sweat, and is fully willing to be intense about their workout. All of the no-nos are gone forever. Tobacco, soda, fast food – gone – forever. (This includes sweet tea as well.) Alcohol is limited and if it curtails your workout in any way – alcohol is gone too. Artificial sweeteners are not tolerated – gone.

I am going to interject a small section on failing the wrong way here (I wish I were done with failing the wrong way, but it is way too prevalent.) I have had the opportunity to watch many people come to the gym with intentions to prove that something is better than nothing. They will ease into it. They will do a little more each day. It will come around and when so and so joins, they will get into it then. You know, not very serious and full of excuses.

My belief is that this population views themselves as able to turn it on when they need to. That nothing can stand in their way and success is entirely up to them. They have done this in their work life, family life, etc. What can be so hard? And, if it doesn't work out, they're not the only one and that's what doctors are for. Right?

I'm sorry to say that these people never succeed. This tepid approach leads to disappointments and, ultimately to a belief that it cannot be done for them. They have "realized" that they are different. That somehow the other 7 Billion people can have what they cannot. Really?

What I really want to say is – This is not an "it." A 100% effort on your part is not too much to ask. This is *your* health that we are talking about. *Your* future ability to do what you want to does depend on *your* efforts to succeed. This transformation probably will take longer than you wish it to. You are not different. It will be harder than you want it to be. It will probably cost more than you expected. On and on. Sorry.

The good news – there is not a finish line. The more you go, the harder you try, the more you pay attention to your sleep and nutrition – the better you will become. Relying on medications, diets, magical cures, etc., is gone. The benefits of being healthy and fit are too numerous to mention, and they are somewhat different for each of us. You honestly doing your best is what it takes. And here is a beautiful caveat – being healthy is way cheaper than not.

To get this thing started, please follow the steps, and get a confidant first. The gym owner may be the right person or able to help you select one. Do not doubt this step and try to go it alone. Understand that you are at the spot that you're in and that *you* did it. Accept this responsibility and choose wisely. Realize that those around you probably helped you get to where you are, so do not ask them. Learn to recognize the problem and to be severely honest with yourself. You should not dump those around you, just choose when to listen to them.

Your goal is to get to the right spot within six months. Do not be the one who says that you can do it cheaper if you just took seven, eight, etc. months. Get this done in six months. Forget the money. You are too important. A confidant will help you to succeed.

Why six months? Six months is enough time for you to experience a large portion of the rewards from your effort and to get through the bumps that you will face.

Why a gym? This would be a great question if you are self-disciplined, but I am assuming that you are not. The gym provides an atmosphere that should focus YOU on YOU. What I tell people is that you cannot do your dishes or laundry at the gym. You may as well get to work and get healthy.

By all means if you have another venue where you can honestly focus (and your confidant agrees), go there.

Where does the fail part come in?

To get this work seriously on its way in six months means that you are going to push your envelope in ways that you have not seen nor thought possible. With this "go-for-it" approach, you will need to accept that you will not always be successful. This is more than OK. This is how you want it to be. Laugh! It is very powerful to not take yourself seriously. You have a long way to go. Let me explain with an unrelated example that may be familiar to you:

Let's say that you are given a task that you are used to and you succeed at completing that task – did you really grow? Are you better than before? The answer is – not really, you just did what you already knew how to do and a short congratulations may be in order and maybe not even that. So freaking what.

Now what if you are given a task that you are not used to and you have the added pressure that you need to succeed? How do you handle that? You learn what you can and then try! That is what you do! Sometimes this effort does not turn out successfully. Here is where you question yourself and wonder if you're on the right track or in over your head (By the way, you are on the right track, and you are not in over your head.) Do your best and accept that you may not complete the task successfully. You may feel like you failed. Oops. Did you do your best? Yes? Then laugh at yourself and try to find a way to be successful. No harm, no foul. It's a task that you were not familiar with. You knew that going in. There is tomorrow. You are fine. You will grow from this experience and be better for it! Let's say that the answer is no, you didn't do your best. Is this bad? No. You were honest with yourself and now you just need to learn from this experience. At the end of the day, though, you need to succeed. Having the need to succeed means that you cannot stop.

The same is to be said regarding fitness. If you do something well and do not get out of your comfort zone, did you really improve or just go through some motions? What is the point? Do you really expect anything to change? (Please say no.)

What if you are given a fitness routine that you are not familiar with or it is harder than you believe you are capable of doing, and you have the added pressure that you have to succeed? How do you handle that? The right answer is to safely try and make sure to safely try your best. Chances are that you will not succeed at first. And here is the good news: Your body will sense this "failure" and adapt to this challenge.

Your body is a brilliant piece of equipment that will self-evaluate any task you give it. If the answer is yes, and it should be, the body will respond by getting stronger at the challenge. It wants you to succeed and will try to make it happen. Your willpower is the key. Make this a motivated challenge and get with the right coach and succeed! You are right. This is hard, and also this is where you can change. You will have to learn an improved technique and work harder. Awesome! Six months and you will be a believer.

An example that you will understand is jogging. If you are not a mobile person now but want to jog, then your first experience out may not be your most fun (There is a great chance it'll suck). You will probably be out of breath quickly. Your heart may feel like it's bouncing out of your chest. Your knees hurt, etc. Awful! Your jog quickly turns into a walk/jog and then finally a walk. You may feel defeated and want to quit but the caveat is that you *need* to succeed. Don't give yourself a choice. All kinds of negative thoughts will be going through your head. You have no choice but to ignore them. Remember the caveat. Keep going. What you are experiencing is a transition to a better you, and it's not pleasant. You may be feeling like a failure (remember the title of the chapter – here you are), but keep the long view and keep going. Your diet may have to change (to the better), you may have to sleep more (good), you may lose weight (what's wrong with that?), etc. This will be hard (suck) in the beginning but will get better as you go. Keep it up and seek any honest positive motivation! Keep an "I need this for ME!" attitude.

Now fast forward several weeks of this type of steady effort and all of a sudden you are able to complete your goal distance with only minor issues. What happened? Answer: Your body adapted and now you can add to this success. Basically, failure became success! (THIS is the point of the chapter.) You are now better overall! There are only a couple of things left for you to understand. 1: That you are never done. You can always get better, but for crying out loud – keep it up! If you do stop, it is very important for you to understand that you will spiral down much faster than you climbed up. And 2: This approach is not limited to jogging. It occurs for all challenges where you are "in over your head" and consistent with your effort to succeed. The key to your success is continued effort combined with continued challenges.

One of the main keys that is imbedded in the preceding paragraphs and I want to be blatant about it: I am speaking about the need for you to be "in over your head." Just outside of your grasp is the sweet spot. This is very important to success as well as the point that you can never be satisfied with yourself. These six months will transform you if you keep the hammer down. Be greedy with your goals. Reach out there, and go for the gold!

I believe that you can see the win-win opportunity here. You will gain major confidence and your body will be the one you have been after for a long time! Confidence will breed confidence as well as the right type of failure will breed success.

OK – How do I do this? Great question.

Get with your confidant, check with your doctor, and then get going. Each day that you put off this transition is only making your change harder to achieve. Why would you do this? Doing the right thing is the right thing at all times and this never changes!

If you get a "hold on a minute" from your doctor, and you need to accomplish some milestones to be allowed to exercise – do it. As soon as you are cleared for exercise, get to work! Full steam ahead. Try not to look up for six months. The clock starts when your exercise effort does. Get your nutrition right immediately and capture those benefits! Please enjoy your journey, but don't take your eye off the ball. Go!

How? This is an important point. Be very picky and choose a confidant that does not want to hear your BS about how bad stuff hurts, your back or any of the other malarkey that you can dream up to slow your progress. You will have issues. I promise you that. You need someone who cares enough for you to listen for the real issues and to ignore the

BS. This person is a key to success. I hope they push you to where you do not believe that you can go.

If you cannot find a confidant quickly, understand that you are at a point in your life where you want to succeed. Confidant or not. Get going. Select a personal trainer that will drive you to succeed physically, to eat right and keep looking for the right confidant. There are no reasons to hesitate. The six-month timeframe does not change either. Once you take the first step, the clock starts. Keep the hammer safely down.

This is also the point of data collection. Measure yourself with performance measures. How much can you bench? How fast can you run/walk a mile? Can you get off the floor by yourself? Whatever is important to you, please measure it and use this information as motivational tools. Remember that your goal is yours. Be confident that YOU matter.

If this helps, take pictures so you can see the difference and then watch it happen! I don't care what you choose to help you. Your body is yours. Get going.

Weight is a point that people focus on. Sure you can weigh yourself. Please do. You want to know, but do not make this about weight. Weight will take care of itself if you focus on nutrition and exercise. Six months from now you will weigh what you need to weigh, and you will also understand what I am talking about. I'm on the page of "who gives a crap about weight." You matter – not a number on a scale.

What not to do? Do not make this about vanity. You will never be satisfied as you will be wanting to please others and will spend an inordinate amount of time trying to figure out what others are thinking. YOU matter – not *their* opinions.

On this point, I had a conversation with a trainer who works for me. I asked her why she got into fitness and her answer was basically to do her best to look like what a guy would want her to look like. And she went down that path. I then asked her what would have happened if a guy would have criticized her progress and the answer was that she would have been devastated and stopped. Basically, her goal wasn't hers – it was the opinion of others. Screw them.

What the general public views as beautiful today is vanity based and not very enduring nor valid. As we get older, we will physically be more vulnerable and heal slower. OK. Knowing that leads me to this definition of beautiful: beautiful to me focuses on an individual who strives to truly stay healthy and exhibits a passion towards helping others regardless of their situation.

So for the trainer to get motivated, she needed to change her goals to better ones. She made her transformation about herself and not others, and now she's successful and does some pretty cool stuff too.

The negatives that she faces today are ones that you might expect. She gets asked if she is still doing that healthy crap. She gets told that she is too skinny, too bulky, too strong, blah, blah, blah. These comments come from both sexes. And she has completely realized that these comments only come from people who are selfish and not confident in their own lives and who want to bring her down to their level. No thanks.

You will likely face these comments from friends, relatives, acquaintances, strangers, etc. As you get older and the people around you age, they also will try to bring you down so they don't look or feel so bad.

My advice: Ignore all of them. You're you and YOU matter. Please get going.

Enough of that tirade. What do you do? What are the steps? What does this look like?

Confidant or not, get going! Get with a trainer who you trust and start. Your workouts need to matter. Forget about the start slow and ease into its stuff. I've seen enough of people who believe that something is better than nothing. I am firmly on the page that, something is the same as nothing.

I'm being redundant, but get going for real! You know yourself, be honest. If your workouts do not seem to be significantly changing you, then they are not! Make it matter!

What you do first is to get over yourself. This change to you will be dramatic and more than likely uncomfortable. I'm sorry but I already know it hurts. I understand that you will have doubts about your direction. You will have others tell you that you are OK as you are (don't listen to them). The early days of this experience are going to suck. In six months, a wonderful thing will have happened to you! You will have lost fat, gained muscle, improved stamina, gained strength, improved confidence, etc. Six lousy months is a reasonable amount of time. This is a great investment. Do it!

And here is what matters next – keep going. As long as you are doing this safely and your discomfort is bearable, you are not going to get hurt. You're fine. Don't worry about it. Remember this: It is nice to be where it's comfortable, but nothing ever changes there. You want change? Then it's up to you to charge ahead. Take this discomfort and accept it. If you are needing confirmation that all is OK, purchase a heart rate monitor. Choose to be at 80% of your theoretical max. It's easy to figure. Use this formula: 220 minus your age, multiplied by 8. You should be in that range for 30 minutes a day and probably six days per week.

More redundancy: Please fail! Who spouts these words? Only those who want you to honestly succeed – that's who. Your experience can easily be broadened if you choose to push your boundaries. The idea that we should succeed each time we try a new venture is silly. We know this. How many times have we discovered that we suck at something the first time out and then go on to discover that we do actually got better as we went along? Then we discover that we enjoy the challenge.

Failure is just a step in the process as it provides a venue for us to learn to get better and in the process of getting better at something, we tend to get better all the way around. Awesome!

This does not mean that we should not back away from any challenges. There are things that we will never be able to do, and there is a larger list of things that we just cannot do yet. Choosing your battles and their sequencing is vital to your ultimate conversion from failure to success. I am encouraging you to discuss each new physical opportunity with your confidant to see if it pushes you but is within your grasp if you choose to reach for it.

An easy example for me is that I wanted to Power Clean 135 lbs. I basically couldn't get the bar above my hips.

Stepping back and looking at this challenge had me realize that I was weak in other moves that, with planning and effort, I could strengthen. After these weaknesses were improved, I can now Power Clean 150 lbs. and sincerely want 165 lbs. And now, I not only have the Power Clean I wanted, I am also better in other venues as well. This was a worthwhile fail. I'm happier.

Kids: The first thing to do as a parent is to set an example of how healthy living should look. You are right that your kids are first and take priority in your lives. That is my point. With them being first, you have to show them the right way to do things and this means being a parent and not just a friend. Your need to do things right accelerates with kids in your life. What I see is that kids become an excuse for bad living and delaying your improvements when the reverse should be true. Eat well and be active! You're happier, and they will see and mimic you. What better gift can you offer your children that a healthy life?

When your children get involved in activities, they will understand that they will suffer failures. How these are handled by you matters. Usually, get up, brush yourself off and get going is what needs to be said. Do not be a helicopter parent. Let them fail safely. The learning they will achieve will carry them throughout their lives. Coach them, but let them take some lumps. They will win and ultimately be thankful for your trust in them.

The amount of latitude you offer needs to adjust with the age of the child. In their early years, you will need to offer a little more hand-holding. Spend your time and effort early. They are just like you in that they learn the best and retain the most at the earliest stages of life. As they move into their middle school, high school, college days, their independence will take hold and parents matter less. Use your time when it counts the most.

If you're reading this book in the years that your children are a little older, don't despair as your role has changed. Now you need to really pay attention and keep communication lines open with them. Understand that their pride may keep them from telling you what is wrong. It is important that they know that you went through those same years and took some knocks yourself (We all did.) Open up to them and tell them your stories. The dumber, the better. Reveal to them that you were human once, and you will develop a level of respect that will keep open communication and you can then honestly help them. They will trust you more if you show your weaknesses to them.

Basically, if you smoked dope, got detention, wrecked a car, got an F on a test, picked last at a sport, cut from a team, etc., tell them about it. We all did something that we're less than proud of. So tell them and laugh at how little it really matters now. Of course you need to tell them to not do the stupid crap you did but life does go on. Do your best and convey to them that tomorrow does exist and matters.

Conclusion

There are two types of failure. A bad approach to failure is based in the myth that you do not matter. You do matter, and now I'm asking you to act like it. Do not become an excuse machine and let life lead you. Please lead life and be willing to take chances to succeed and define success in ways that lead you to a healthier lifestyle. Discount genetics and fate as determinants in your life. You are in charge – no one else. Accept illnesses as a choice and a self-created problem and do something about it. You very seldom have to be sick. If you are, find out why and fix it!

Understand that your choices will not all work out and may lead you down a different path. OK. Without trying, you never would have known. In this vein, a confidant becomes even more important so that you get positive feedback towards your goals and the shortcomings of your approach.

For your kids: Be vulnerable and show them what true effort looks like. Laugh with them so they are not afraid to try. Life sucks sometimes. Let them know that this is OK. Show them how to handle life for whatever it hands them. Their life lessons come from you. Never forget that.

For me – as I move through life – I understand that the challenges I face need to be met from a comprehensive solution approach. Steps from A to B usually require Steps A.1+A.2+A.3 etc. in order to accomplish the challenge and finally get to B. Although I wanted the solution to be easier, I try not to short circuit the steps nor believe that easy really works. I have come to expect and even delight in the failing of some or all of the steps towards an honest goal as I am aware that each failure improves me in the category that I am seeking and consequential improvements elsewhere within me. Only through failure do I learn these things.

Chapter Eight
Nutrition

Nutrition is really a straightforward concept in that it's easy. Choose lots of fruits and vegetables, some grain, a little meat and go very easy on the sugar and off you go. Eat for the sake of physical and mental performance, and you will do very well.

The simpler the better. If you can pronounce the ingredients and understand all that goes into producing it, it's OK to eat it. Do not worry about quantity. Food is not a discipline that should be allowed to be complicated in your life. There's too much already. The trick I've found to be most useful is to create a circle of Good Food Items (GFI) and be very selective in what goes into this grouping.

I am trying to be only positive in this book and trying to keep all information simple. One area that makes this approach hard has to do with fad diets. The word diet is offensive in that in generally involves biased restrictions. This means that success be fleeting and will leave you with a metabolic mess that may take years to overcome. If you are even able to overcome it. They are usually that bad.

When a diet claims "amazing" results in a short amount of time, the diet is also referring to short-term success.

Sustainability and satisfaction are required for success. Many diets today come from the internet and have caveats in the fine print which reveal them as a hoax.

Many diets require a shortage of nutrition and use the verbiage calorie and nutrition interchangeably. You need sufficient nutrition daily – period. The idea that you can come up short on nutrition and that your body won't mind is silly. Your body is a series of chemical reactions. If you leave out nutrition, the reactions will be negatively altered and create a shortfall within you that will eventually cause you serious problems and is not sustainable. All energy that is delivered to your body is converted to adenosine triphosphate (ATP). This energy is initially the blast you feel when you get excited. After this blast, your body needs to convert stored energy into ATP for usage. Your body uses energy in this order: Carbohydrates are converted to ATP (good carbs). In the early stages of energy consumption, carbs are used to power you. When you have completed this energy store, then your body will move to protein.

Protein is second on the list. If you have physical demands on your body that extends past your carbohydrate store, then your body will choose from available protein and convert it to ATP for usage. If not available through good food, your body will pull energy from muscle which will leave you very weak. Fat is the tricky one. The use of fat for energy is what most of us want. If you are out of carbs and protein and your body believes that more nutrition will become available, your body will then gravitate to fat as an energy source. Another reason that your body will choose fat as its energy source is when you require a consistent, slow feed of energy (such as a long slow jog, a long easy bike ride, gentle laps in the pool, etc.).

Many believe in the "calorie in, calorie out" myth. Your body needs energy to survive and will get it from the easiest source available. When you place a demand on your body and do not eat enough real food, your body will satisfy the demand the easiest way it can. Eat enough real food, and you will do fine. You will complete your task and have more than enough energy. Do not eat enough and your body will pull energy from muscle before moving on to fat. This is why many people who are "dieting" find themselves extremely weak and just assume that it's the price of losing weight. You should become stronger as you lose weight. If you are not getting stronger as you progress through your efforts then immediately check with your confidant and get on the right track. Your only acceptable result from this effort is to become stronger.

The appropriate way to lose weight requires enough good food and exercise to be successful. A simple visual would be to view food as fuel and exercise as a continuous "match." Basically, start a fire and keep it burning. If you do not have the fuel the fire will go out. If you do not have the match, the fire doesn't start. If you do not repeatedly light the fire, it will go out.

Light the fire, keep feeding the fire and keep lighting the fire. This approach should never stop.

Make good food convenient. Have fruit, dark chocolate, and other healthy snacks easily available. Never have a reason to be hungry without easy access to good food. Do not remain hungry for long as the easy answers will come to mind more quickly than the better ones.

A very important answer to eating involves a solid strategy towards food preparation. You already know that you will eat this week. No surprise there. What is a smart way to go about it?

Meal preparation is very worthwhile. Cut your vegetables, brown your meat, soak your beans, etc. on a day that you have plenty of time. A little bulk planning will leave you quite an opportunity to assemble a breakfast, lunch or dinner offering that is good for you. You'll be surprised at your creativity if you have several foods prepped and easy for you to finish into a wonderful dish. Take the time (it's really not that much) and enjoy the benefits.

Make bad food inconvenient. Don't keep it at your house. For instance, only buy ice cream at restaurants. If it's expensive and inconvenient, you will seldom choose it.

Good food and exercise are required for successful weight loss. Any "promise" to thwart this reality sets you back and makes the process harder. Start today and do not stop.

Basic understandings are required for nutrition success. Complicated has little role in this battle. I'll try to cover the categories that should be considered. The order of importance is more up to the reader than the author so choose what's important to you. Go with it and evolve with it.

Organic versus non-organic. Organic! Every time. This concept comes from a serious distrust by us of the chemical industry and their lack of meaningful regulation or testing. The common argument is that the cost of organic is higher. What is honestly meant is that the price is higher, not the cost. Price and cost frequently do not relate to each other. Disease is as much or more of a choice than chance. While the price of avoiding disease is higher than taking the chance, the cost of repairing disease is always high and sometimes not even doable. Organic food may not in itself prevent disease but take all of the help you can get. Choose to believe that you can beat the odds and not get a disease. This takes meaningful steps and choosing organic is one of them.

How many calories should I eat? This is an interesting topic. The first answer that comes to mind is – as many as you need. View food as fuel and you cannot go wrong. The solution to getting healthy is comprehensive. The number of calories needed is fully tied to your success with activity, sleep, stress, etc. Getting caught in a mindset that a set number exists somewhere that works for every/anyone isn't true. If you begin to find success with activity, you will need more calories. The value of choosing of good calories far outweighs the number of them. The intensity of your activity is your best indicator of your food needs. Keep high expectations for your performance and study the effects of your food selections.

An example would be if you plan to complete a 5K and the morning of the run you are hungry. If you eat a fast food breakfast, I suspect that your performance will not be good. This experience has little to do with calorie quantity but food selection. Choose wisely and let your ability to be intense determine if you are right or not. If you can give an all-out effort, you've chosen wisely. Simple as that. I use a rule that if I'm about to indulge in an exercise activity and feel a hunger, I satisfy it prior to moving forward. I do not eat much – ½ burrito, ½ PB&J – just enough to stop the hunger, and I go to work. Keep your answer handy as you know when you are going to be active so be prepared and willing to eat if necessary. Then after you are finished exercising, finish eating and feel good about it. Do you need a protein shake to repair you muscles? Not really. You should eat easily digestible protein and about fifteen to twenty grams of it. Peanut butter, nuts, a couple of boiled eggs, etc. Easy food. Eat healthy, eat enough, and move on!

What foods should I include and what foods should I avoid? Let's explain a concept that we call Good Food Items (GFI). What is GFI? This is a selective list of items that you KNOW are good. Make one for you. This is a great time to have an in-depth discussion with your confidant, doctor, family, and yourself. Make a list of rules for you to include any known allergies or other ill effects from food. All food that violate these rules are excluded automatically from YOUR list. No exceptions. Now make a list of food that you know to be good for you. Fruits and vegetables are easy to be on top and should comprise most of your plate anyway. Any beans that do not give you issues, add them. Lean meats that are grass fed, organic – OK. Make the list yours and apply them to all eating opportunities. Processed foods – no. Leave them off and never add them. Organic processed foods? Leave them out. Be very selective as to what goes on the list and very liberal on what does not. Expand the list as you find good foods that you like. As you complete the setup of this list, eat what you want from it. Feel free to indulge! If you find problems with any item on the list, dismiss it and/or categorize it to a seldom-consumed item. You are in charge. Do not under eat but use your ability to give an all-out effort as a true guide to fill your plate. Prioritize your performance over food and you will do well.

When you go grocery shopping, use this list as a refill job. Make sure that you have enough on hand to complete any dish that you like but not too much that spoilage is a concern. Dried foods purchased in bulk are great in that they last a long time, are easy to fix, versatility is high, and the cost is low. Some advice regarding finding low-cost satiation – spices. Take any bland food that is good for you and spice it up. You'll eat less and be more satisfied if you do. Turmeric, curry powder, garlic powder, etc. All are reasonably low cost as a little bit goes a long way. Make food taste as you want it to so that you're not searching for fulfilment through volume.

You will find that your food cost will diminish significantly through this approach as whole foods tend to not cost a lot and their versatility allows you to be creative.

How many times a day should I eat? This again is a simple answer: Use your ability to exert a strong effort to guide your food intake. Do all that you can to optimize your performance and nutrition will automatically correct itself. If you find that you are hungry, eat. If this means ten times a day, let us get out of your way so that you succeed. If this means three times a day, let us get out of your way so that you succeed. See the difference? Your success is what is important and not rules. The only advice that we will offer is to eat at a minimum of three meals a day. Any less than this is inviting your body to feel sluggish as it is forced to digest oversized portions of food at untimely parts of the day. Eating a minimum of three meals a day should allow you to space these meals out so that your performance is optimized. Always consider your performance as your guide. You want the most physically out of yourself.

I need sweets! Help me! Not a problem! I eat them too. Just use your effort as stated in previous paragraphs and you will do fine. If/when you over eat sweets, your performance will suffer and then correct your intake. Take note that sweets are last on your true needs list so if you need to correct: start here first. Do not eliminate sweets if you love them. Just make sure they are placed properly in your priority list. This is the same rule as alcohol. Your ability to provide a strong effort is paramount. Do not deviate and you will do fine.

How much protein do I need? I do not know. Usually between sixty and one hundred grams per day. Understand that protein cannot be stored in the body. Any excess needs to be processed by your kidneys and most eliminated through urination with some converted and stored as fat. Understand that long term excesses of protein can and will cause kidney issues. You are right in that you need protein to repair and build muscle. So choose non-animal protein first. This means beans, eggs, and other legumes. Non-animal protein is easy to digest and allows for faster muscle cell repair. If you must eat animal protein, then choose grass fed, zero hormone, no antibiotic meat. Kind of hard to find and the price is higher but worth the search as your body will love you for it.

What should I drink? This is an important category as a lot of meaningless calories come from beverages. Choose carefully and as close to water as you can. I've heard many say that they do not like water and I've always wondered why? The best answer that I can come up with is that our taste buds have been trained to prefer choices that are not very good for you. Your taste buds can and should be trained for your benefit. Unsweetened beverages are best. Artificial sweeteners are not good substitutes. Let the need for sweet diminish to a healthy level. This advice might seem painful but it's really not.

To specify a little bit with the goal of getting you on the right page, I offer the following:

Water – yes.

Coffee, organic and without sweeteners or milk – yes.

Tea – no sweeteners – yes – iced or hot.

Milk – almond, rice, coconut – yes; animal milk – limited.

Juices – pretty much no – way too much sugar.

Soda – never under any circumstances.

Alcohol – very limited – choose the good stuff and keep the volume limited.

Protein shakes – just if you want to – don't rely on them for their proposed effects.

Meal replacement drinks – never unless under a doctor's care. A warning here: do not get caught in the idea that there is an easy answer – it doesn't exist and never will.

I believe that these are guidelines to direct your evaluation of drinks. The best advice that I can give is to choose what goes into your GFI here as well. Be very honest with yourself and selective on what goes into your list and you'll do fine.

"When I go to a pitch-in, the food is all bad. What do I do?" You should view this as an opportunity to shine. Bring a healthy selection with enough to share. Assume that others want healthy options just as you do. This dish can be a great conversation starter.

One topic to discuss is food marketing. A sincere goal of mine with this book is not to be "preachy." Food marketing is an area where I may cross that line.

For decades we have been told that we have free choice in our food selections and while this is technically true, we need to understand that food companies spend untold amounts of money on marketing to convince you that you and your family will be happier and more satisfied if you add their products to your life. This marketing holds nothing back in their appeal including claims/phrases such as: low price, healthy, low calorie, happy, fun, kids, social, good value, big servings, salad bars, convenient, coupons, fundraisers. They do everything they can do to bring you to their door. Basically, they are doing all they can to deny your free will.

Marketing is a large component of the price in grocery stores too. When you see a box, can, or bottle dolled up telling you great things – be wary. Usually it's just a cover up of the cheap ingredients within. Use the advice stated above in grocery stores: If you cannot pronounce it and or do not know the full story on where the food came from, do not buy it. And keep it this simple.

As you learn, you may discover that some items are good and should be added to your GFI and some are not and should be removed. Keep the list dynamic to allow for this information. Our lives are an evolution, and always will be. Be very willing to adapt to it. Just make sure that you choose healthy at all times.

I see many examples of people angry that grocery food pricing is increasing and that they cannot afford to eat. Yet while they are complaining, I discover they just came back from a restaurant or the gas station? It's hard to argue that we get a lot of calories from convenient stores. We should stop.

An important area of concern is peer pressure. This comes in the form of family, friends, co-workers, company events, etc. Well-intentioned acquaintances will not be satisfied until they see you eat according to their wishes and values. This means desserts usually. These moments are very uncomfortable so what do you do?

First, use all of your communication avenues to convey that you are taking charge of your life and are seeking everyone's cooperation. When the pushy aunt insists that you eat their cake, you now have something to point to that shifts the paradigm and then seek that person's help in achieving your goal to live a healthy life. Don't take no for an answer.

Second, keep your communication going. As you succeed, be sure and tell others. This will have several effects. It will help you be more accountable to yourself and give you more answers for when the temptations come.

Third, when this group tries to make you uncomfortable for "judging" their offering as unhealthy, keep your responses simple and just state that you feel great and thank them for caring and let it go at that. Don't take the bait to indulge in a long conversation where you could inadvertently say something that will be used against you. Change the subject, and do what you need to do.

OK. You gave in and ate some food that you knew wasn't good for you. At least recognize that you did it. You'll live. Don't make a habit of it. Get back on track and move on.

What should I do regarding desserts? Temptations are everywhere. What is the plan?

We all like desserts. Efforts to only eat fruit to satisfy our sweet tooth is a miserable failure. We need more! And, here is the but – I work to make my own so that I know what goes in to making it. When I make a pie, I use whole wheat flour for the crust. I reduce the sugar and add slightly more of spices that I like. Cinnamon is an easy favorite for me for most pies. With cakes, use whole wheat flour. Add a little more baking powder and who will know. I've developed a taste for dark chocolate. You will eat less of it as it's much more satisfying, and you will get an antioxidant effect as well. Be thoughtful in your approach to dessert and you will do fine. Make it a once a week occurrence. Another approach that I employ is to only eat desserts at restaurants, and make sure that I pay too much for them. It doesn't take many six-dollar scoops of ice cream to learn to say no. My body and billfold both wins.

What should I do regarding snacks? I get hungry sometimes and just want to snack. First, this happens to all of us. Everyday. What you do about it is what is important. The answer is really pretty simple in that you just use your GFI and satisfy your "wants."

The development of your GFI is not a short-term limited use item. The concept is that any and all calories entering your body should come from this list. This list is yours!

Make it one that you are satisfied with and that it is comprehensive enough to cover snacks as well.

Categorize your list into the following sections:
Meats
Vegetables
Fruits
Grains
Desserts
Snacks
Beverages

Now fill in what should go into your Good Food Items list per section and you are on your way!

Does any of this really matter? I'm already exercising right?

The answer is an emphatic yes! By taking the steps to become healthy and active, you have chosen to be serious! This is awesome! Be serious for six months, and then realize that you are right. This was all worthwhile, and you will not understand what took you so long to come to this realization. Eating healthy is more than just complementary to exercise. Eating healthy is a *requirement* of being healthy. You are worth it!

What if I continue to eat as I always have? Everyone else is doing it. If you are eating good healthy food now, not a problem. If you are eating crap, then please change. Our bodies are basically chemical reactions that occur due to the stimuli given to them. This comes in the form of stress, exercise, sleep, living, etc. If you give your body junk, please expect bad to happen with zero chance of a healthy outcome. If you give your body good food, please expect a much higher chance of a healthy outcome, but it is not a certainty. You still need the other components of health to achieve success.

A really important conversation needs to be had regarding sugar. I have been around long enough to have watched the ebb and flow of information dictating good and bad foods. I have watched protein make its way into shampoo and cholesterol get blasted from all sides. Fat is being made out as the cause of obesity and now fat free will somehow repair your life and make you famous? Some of this misinformation is "harmless" marketing. Really? A high protein shampoo is to do what? Some of this is downright dangerous. The fat-free food rage created a monster. When fat was removed from food (because eating fat makes you fat?), food tasted horrible and so sugar was added. Because sugar is low calorie – and if you follow the calorie is a calorie myth – the approach seemed harmless. Since the removal of fat from food offerings (or because of it), our waistlines have ballooned out of hand. No doubt that there are really bad fats, and we need to stay away from them. Omega-3 fatty acids are good. Monounsaturated fats – yep. Polyunsaturated fats – yep. Saturated fats – some. Trans fats – NEVER. As you can see, most fats have value and the one that is 100% manmade and found in processed food is awful. Stay away!

Do some research and you will be happy to know that eating food that is good is also good for you.

And now for sugar. I struggle to think of a nutrition based good word for the stuff (and I like it). Please do not misunderstand me. There are good sugars. These are the ones that are located within whole fruit. The reason for this allowance is that sugar found within fruit is surrounded by fiber. This fiber slows the digestive process down preventing the pancreas from releasing insulin and allowing the sugar to be directly used as energy. OK! Eat fruit!

On the other hand, the majority of added sugar it is not surrounded by fiber and heads straight into the digestive system with nowhere to go. Your pancreas freaks out and releases insulin so that the sugar can get out of your blood. Where does it go? TO YOUR FAT! That's where. And this is why a calorie is not a calorie. Remember the energy usage flow from earlier? Carbs first, protein second, and fat last. The fat that was just added to your body will be some of the last energy that your body will use.

Our bodies can typically process between seven – nine teaspoons of sugar daily. As Americans, we are consuming approximately nineteen teaspoons of sugar daily! This is not a zero-sum game where it is just information that you have heard before, and you can claim to try to do better. Please understand that ten extra teaspoons per day means that 3,650 teaspoons per year is over-consumed and over ten years, 36,500 teaspoons will be over-consumed. The damage this creates is devastating in terms of type 2 diabetes which leads to high health care costs and very much more importantly: lost eyesight, amputations, cancer, high blood pressure, osteoarthritis, gout, non-alcoholic fatty liver disease, heart disease, etc. Sugar making food taste good does not warrant this amount of damage. Having type 2 diabetes is a choice. This statement will upset several, but too bad. Your genetics may contribute to type 2 diabetes but you can overcome that with proper nutrition. Choosing not to have proper nutrition and getting sick is a choice.

What do you do? Stop using the stuff! Your taste buds will change to support your new approach. Here is an example that I personally witnessed while in Japan in 1995. I was in a grocery store in Kariya City and was in the checkout lane. The checkout lanes in Japan are very similar to ours in that they also tempt you with last second purchases of treats just prior to the cash register. You know the ones that you see little kids crying to their parents that they need to survive. We instantly think of it as a last second attempt to sell candy. What I witnessed was a little boy (about five years old) crying to his mom that he "needed" this treat, and the mom was telling him, "No, no. Put it back." He reluctantly did. After they made their purchase, I was nosy and picked up the "needed" treat. It was a rice cracker wrapped by seaweed. I learned then and there that the love of sweet things is a learned behavior and not natural. That five-year-old kid was not making a political statement about his sugar intake. No, he wanted a treat and that is all. His taste buds are the way they are intended to be. Ours have been manipulated by food scientists to require sweet.

Change them back and watch your health outcome improve dramatically.

Water: We know that we need it. What are the parameters around it? Take your weight in pounds and then divide the number by two to get the number of ounces needed. You do need to adjust to a higher level when you exercise. A great rule of thumb is if you're thirsty, then drink. If you are running outside, then drink early and drink often. Do not get dehydrated

Another rule of thumb is to look at the color of your urine which should be slightly colored. If it is too yellow, then you are probably dehydrated and should drink. If it is too clear, then you are probably overhydrated and risk flushing out necessary minerals from your body. Do you best to keep it slightly colored and you should be fine.

Chapter Nine
Exercise

From my early childhood (beginning in 1975) through late 2010, exercise has been an easy part of my life. I just ran. I ran for the heck of it. I ran to prepare for races of 800 meters through the marathon. I ran on tracks, country roads, trails, grass, hills, and flat. I ran because I liked it. I've completed six marathons, many half marathons and countless 10Ks and 5Ks. I've also completed two Spartan Trifectas. I started bicycling as well and have a 160-mile one-day ride, a few MS150's and a Hilly Hundred completed. I've put a lot of emphasis on cardio, and I enjoy it.

In 2010, I decided to purchase a fitness franchise and became aware of the world of equipment. Cardio machines and a variety of weight lifting devices became a part of my life. I began my franchise in August 2010 and spent the first year trying to fit in with my customers. I tried to lift weights, use protein powder – you know, the chest/back days followed by leg days, etc. I learned reasonably quickly that this approach leads to very little in the way of health or tangible benefits.

Also, I have spent the last nine years learning about the motivations of a wide array of the customer base and, quite frankly, am not surprised at the sad state of health of Americans. While a few use my fitness center to get healthy – most attempt to use it to lose weight and/or to get back to their high school glory days (usually 10-30 years ago).

What I have discovered is that most people rely on bad information, poor attitudes, and low-price mindsets. You know, the I-have-to-have-it-now mindsets, etc. – trying to overcome decades of unhealthy living.

While everyone wants to think of themselves as goal driven and serious towards their health, the reality is different. Somehow our mindset is that health is simply the absence of injury or illness. This needs to change. Health should be defined as the unmistakable ability to attempt any feat you desire. Little should be outside of your realm. If you want to ride a bike, play with your kids/grandkids, hike, badminton – at whatever age you are – you should be fit enough to do it. Doubt or fear of a catastrophic health crisis should be the furthest from your mind.

Our current approach to "health" goals really get down to two things – our weight and the mirror.

While I support that each of us have an ideal weight and how we look will help us define how we feel, I do have issues with these mindsets.

"The less I weigh, the better health I must be in." False. Many follow this idea and it leads to behavioral issues. I watch this mindset transform people from focusing on nutrition to "dieting" (which usually means some new fad diet or even starving themselves). Neither approach works, and both are dangerous. Fad dieting usually does not satisfy for very long and leads to the yo-yo effect which unmistakably worsens the situation. The starvation approach follows the belief that "the less I eat, the less I'll weigh" logic. Your body is a phenomenal machine designed to survive. Fat is our body's defense from starvation and meant to provide you with convertible energy when you have nothing else. By the way, nothing else includes your muscle. If you under eat, your body will actually choose your muscle mass over fat to fuel living. You will get much weaker with this approach.

"If I look good in the mirror, I must be healthy." False. The mirror is meant to be a feedback device to help you get dressed, brush your teeth, etc. Setting your health and fitness goals by your appearance in a mirror leads to constant negativity and a whipsaw approach to your body. Use the mirror as it's intended please.

Using a fitness center to recreate your youth misses the point too. You are where you are. Move forward, and be the best you can be. Set your goal to simply be healthy. Have the unmistakable ability to attempt any feat you desire. If you can sincerely drive yourself towards this goal, you will succeed!

Fitness centers can have the best equipment available on the market, but it's not that simple. Frequency and intensity will drive results. Using the centers casually and hoping for success is an approach but – I need to break it to all of you – it won't happen this way.

1. Let's start with what's wrong (beginning with the equipment itself).

We have to understand that big companies build most of the equipment, and that they have the goal of making the most money possible. The treadmills, ellipticals, stationary bicycles, etc. are marketed as "all you need" to return to your glory days. Of the many issues, intensity and duration come to the top of the list for reasons for failure. The crowd that looks for stationary cardio to change their lives usually are looking for a low-price approach because they know themselves that they are not serious and will only make a "January" attempt to lose weight.

Selectorized equipment are fixed strength machines that focus on one muscle group and can only be used one way. These machines look great and can offer tremendous resistance making you feel like you're progressing. In actuality you're accomplishing little – if any – actual physical gains towards your fitness or health. Often the machines have built in seats that are padded and comfortable which allow too much rest between sets.

Free weight areas of gyms offer versatility in your workout, but for the most part, participants work in the isolated muscle group mode and try to get the biggest bicep, triceps, delt, lat, they can. This can look good in the mirror, but is misleading in regards to being healthy. Often the folks who focus on looks have little in the way of stamina or flexibility.

The folks who are part of the general gym experience struggle getting or being healthy and think that equipment will get them there (wherever "there" is). These folks seem to believe that "something is better than nothing." Hence, they fail. Hard to understand when the "experts" tell you that if you just walk a little more each day, it'll add up and sharply change your health outcomes. The idea that this is silly and you're losing time is a hard pill to swallow.

Add some strength training to your regimen, and you will lose weight. Your HDL and LDL will move to their proper ratios, and you will feel better.

This is the scenario that I've seen. This crowd spends decades living a life that includes horrible eating practices, doesn't exercise, goes from job to job, gets married, divorced, gets into too much debt, has kids – always in a state of transition and never satisfied with themselves – nor anyone around them.

This group by now is in their thirties or forties, and makes a "decision" in January that this is their year to change. So they go to the internet and search for gyms and immediately want to know the price. They already know they're not serious about change and/or they believe that their lives aren't too bad anyway. A small change will transform them to the "stars" they used to be. Sound familiar? Surprised that amazing transitions won't happen?

A lost issue with this approach is this: Years go by and you're now older.

The remedy of these situations takes an understanding of the traps the equipment presents and ignoring them. Any and all of the equipment can be used effectively to achieve health. Properly taught dynamic lifts is the approach needed. The workouts must be based in high intensity for the participant five to six days per week. Use a trusted trainer to make sure that you are set up correctly. Develop and explain your goals to make sure that your plan will be effective.

2. Understand the future. Not many components of the future are predictable. A lot of good and a lot of bad comes

our way in life, and we are reactive to it. We just do our best and move on.

We can, however, put ourselves into a position to control our physical and mental destiny and enjoy it. A positive lifestyle that is comprehensive sets us up for success. When a good opportunity comes along, we are ready to take it. Taking the kids to the park should be an interactive experience. Pickup games should include you. Bicycles are an option. 5K runs, 10K runs, obstacle course races, hiking, etc., are all in play for this group. Helping a neighbor move a couch – no problem. Mowing your grass – OK. A stressful situation comes along – you are ready.

Getting ourselves in place for the future is a basic understanding that the ball is in YOUR hands. It is exciting to know that you have control. As with all things, with great opportunity comes great responsibility. Knowledge is great. Action is greater! Plan and then do.

3. What should be done? It is best to not get into this mess to begin with. We've been told from the get go to take care of ourselves. We should do this. There are many reasons for "getting into the mess," and they're all excuses. Too busy, too expensive, marriage, divorce, kids, poor food choices, smoking, etc. You name it. Learn now and don't make the mistakes. Your whole life will be better for the decision and it's worth it. If you've not made these mistakes, congratulations! Read the rest of the book and glean all of the information you can and keep at it! Everyone else – let's fix this thing.

After the mistakes are made, view the needed changes as a correction to a bad lifestyle and make a new correct lifestyle happen. Throw pride out of the window, laugh at yourself and get to work!

This next comment may well be the most important of your life – You are important enough to make change! Please, please realize this. YOU MATTER!

Realize that a new lifestyle will take a while to generate and will need to be customized to you. A one-size-fits-all approach has a very high probability of failure. I am frequently asked by members, "How many sets and reps do I recommend?" There are too many variables as we are each different people. The real answer is – whatever it takes. Many, many modifications to your first approach are likely. Be patient and willing to adapt. Being healthy is actually pretty easy to understand – just hard to do.

4. What do I do? Some of this has been stated before in this book. I'm OK with repeating it. This is that important.

The highest priority should be to seek help from a qualified confidant. Not everyone fits this bill.

I cannot stress enough that honesty is critical here. No one wants to be unhealthy but here you are. Ask yourself: Why did I do this to myself? What vices do I accept as normal? Am I lazy? Do I eat crap? Am I lazy and eat crap? Do I let a penny get in the way of a dollar? Do not be nice to yourself. You are the only one in your own mind. Tell yourself the truth and be mean. These questions are not trivial. They demand answers from you. Write them down, and then answer them. You are the only one who has to see them. Be honest.

If others love you for who you are, say "So what!" and sincerely decide that a healthy life is for you! Now it's time to choose a confidant. A common error here is to try this on your own. You've spent years, decades, and a lifetime messing up. Face it, you're not qualified to fix this. You need outside help! Get over yourself and get someone. The someone you get has to be honest and sincere and you need to be thorough in your selection process.

If you have self-inflicted medical conditions, please acknowledge them as choices. Do not blame genetics. Type 2 diabetes, high blood pressure, obesity, high cholesterol, sleep apnea, some cancers, etc. These are mainly due to choices that we have made. Blame isn't an answer. Change is!

Change isn't easy. Accept this and understand the magnitude of effort needed to make the change. A direct effort is needed. Do not pussyfoot around and try to shortcut the change. A full-blown effort is needed and much cheaper in the short and long run. And here is what you need to do:

First, accept this little bit of hurtful and challenging advice: Do not choose a friend or relative. A person who doesn't know you and is chosen will guide you honestly – and at this point, you need honesty.

Find a person and interview him/her for your success. Tell him/her your problems and be honest. Who are you, what is wrong with you and what are your weaknesses and perceived strengths. Remember, these people do not know you at all. After full disclosure of who you are (a bit of advice would be to be a little negative on yourself) see if the person has the heart to "adopt" you. Ask yourself – what does it take to fix you. Remember the mean things you thought about yourself. Yes? Will this person tell you the honest truth and resolve your problem? If not, move on.

Honest change can come quickly if you choose wisely. Six months kind of quick!

Understand that this service is needed. ***You Are Worth It.***

Your chosen confidant should immediately begin working with you on a regular basis. Create ALL of the necessary contact information so that communication is frequent and easy. The schedule will appear daunting at the outset so relax and don't become an excuse machine. Understand that this service will cost you – pay it. Do not quibble over a few dollars and lose precious time. A cheap approach at this stage will lead to a probable failure and now you're another year older. Oops!

A great question is "Where do I even look for a potential confidant?"

Shop for a class that engages all fitness levels and will scale your workouts to your ability and then drives you to the edge of your desired ability. High intensity for you will be key to your belief that you're on the right page. Pay attention to the instructor, and see if they care about you. You will know. When you find the class that leaves you breathless, excited, and wanting more, you're on the right track. The instructor of this class may or may not be the right person, but I do believe that if they are not the right person – they will know who is. Shopping for this person is fun as you will get more and more excited about your future as you get closer to the right person.

After you have found the right person, sit down with them and go deep. There are three generic fronts to work on and one is as critical as the next. They are nutrition, sleep and exercise.

Each of these subjects needs to be gone through to their logical conclusion. Please understand that none of this is rocket science, and that if the answer is complicated you may need to move on. Understand that each of these subjects should be used as a disqualifier with the confidant and the applicant able to walk away without fault. I am personally recommending that only one person be your confidant to avoid conflict. But take this selection as life-changing serious. This is an opportunity for you to take full control of your life, and I am hoping that you will do this. Go online to get a life coach if need be. This person does not have to be nearby, and you should understand that they are few and far between. YOU need to win! As you personally become better, you can move this person to a maintenance mode but in the beginning you will need a boss to guide you.

Begin your personal improvement immediately, but do not stop until you have found your confidant.

Now on to your personal improvement.

Let me help set your expectations: Exercise will not make you skinny! I repeat for effect – Exercise will not make you skinny!

Exercise will, however, make you fit, strong, healthier, excrete endorphins to make you happier, make you feel better about yourself, give you energy, and allow you to get into the game of life.

Very important points here: You are not too old, fat, worthless, skinny, young, etc. to exercise. You have to succeed. You will be told that you are OK but fully realize that the people telling you this do NOT have your best interest in mind. Anyone who tells you this may even be trying to control you and love you for who you are. This is so sweet and yet so full of crap. Ignore them and understand that *you are worth it!*

A huge beginning point is to "take it to heart" that this has to become a lifestyle. You are never done. Ever! Please understand and accept this. This is a soapbox moment from me to you. Advice will come from all directions to you and even from you. The only person you should listen to will be your confidant as they should be vested in your success and not your feelings. Feel free to take your concerns, questions, and ideas to him/her but the conclusion of the discovery has to benefit your new lifestyle. No deviations accepted. This is an area of your life that you need to be entirely selfish. Understand that for the next six months or so, living correctly is the game. Do not deviate.

Let's get going. There are six components to a successful exercise program: intensity, duration, form, rest, and longevity, and fun. All are equal in value and meaning.

Let's start with intensity. What is it? Why is it important? How much intensity do I need? Is this safe? Let's go through this:

What is it? There is a phase within personal raining call Rate of Perceived Effort (RPE). It is usually scaled from 1–10. Not a definite measurement method but a very useful communication tool for us. You will be asked to tell us your RPE, and your next step will come from that answer. An answer of 1 basically means you could do this all day, you're bored, what good is this, etc. 10 means that you're over the top – one more rep and then dig a hole, you're done. How much RPE should I exert? This answer is up to you but this comes with an understanding that you will adapt to the effort, and it'll get easier. Accept this and move up in effort. Note that I said effort – not intensity. Keep that the same so you don't become overexerted.

An example could be deadlifts. This is an exercise where you basically see what you can pick up. Let's say that you choose a RPE of six and are asked to Deadlift for five sets at seven repetitions. For this, you choose 100 pounds and succeed and consider the effort a six on the RPE scale. In a few weeks this effort is repeated and you're again asked for five sets of seven but due to your good work you now choose 110 and succeed. Again, you consider the effort a six on the RPE scale.

Awesome! You've adapted to the exercise and have increased your load from 100 to 110 pounds but your RPE (intensity) did not change. Success!

Why is this important? This is important because intensity (RPE) demonstrates to you that you're progressing and it's reasonable and controlled. The RPE scale helps exercise make sense to you and offers a common communication tool between you and your confidant. Please note that the person defining the terms of the scale is you. Your only requirement is to be consistent so that credibility is established from session to session. Basically, you're in charge and the confidant doesn't mind as it's their job to plan for your next step based on the feedback given.

How much Intensity do I need? This is 100% your call. The goal of exercise is to create a lifestyle change that is permanent. Talk to your confidant and have them help you define a reasonable RPE for you and your personality. Some people's personality demonstrates that easy is best. This is fine. This person's progress will be slower but it's OK. Use the RPE scale as its defined. Adapt and move up. Some people's personality show that aggressive is desired. This is fine also. Faster growth will occur and as long as this can be maintained as a new lifestyle – awesome!

Is this safe? With the co-development of the RPE scale between you and your confidant – yes! Follow the plan of keeping the same RPE and grow the results. You will be safe and all of the good benefits will happen from there. You're on your way!

Routine is the enemy to most programming. Keep adding and adjusting your workout to include new and dynamic exercises and then manage the new programming via your RPE.

If your goal is to continually improve and see where you become your best, continue climbing your path until your RPE cannot be maintained. When this happens, talk to your confidant to determine if you should bolster an adjoining muscle group prior to returning to your path. Chances are that you can get better with proper planning.

If you are satisfied with your fitness level then work with your confidant to develop a maintenance approach to your fitness. Make sure that it is varied so that you do not become bored and go backwards.

A sidebar note that I am adding here is a discussion on dynamic versus isolateral exercises. Isolateral exercises focus on singular muscles and tend to be single jointed moves – think bicep curls, triceps extensions and the like. These moves look great in theory but do little for health and fitness. The muscle groups tend to look strong but when challenged are usually not. All show and no go.

I'm an advocate for efficiency. The less time in the gym getting a great workout in the better. Isolateral workouts take up a lot of time that can be used to cover much larger muscle groups. There is good that comes from this type of workout. A benefit is that they are easy to teach and are easy to understand. Also, they are great to allow a longer time in the gym so that the social component of your experience can be fulfilled (You have time to talk to others.)

On the other hand, dynamic moves like Olympic moves, bodyweight exercises, pull-ups, etc., are full body exercises intended to cover many of your muscle groups. These are harder to teach and take an experienced trainer (who may not be your confidant) to help you choose the right weight, methodology, etc. The benefits of dynamic moves are that they improve your body strength and stamina completely and quickly. My vote is always going to be for dynamic exercises.

Next is duration. What is it? Why is it important? How much duration do I need? Is it safe?

What is it? Duration relates to the amount of time and frequency of your efforts. Duration is doing enough so that it matters! Do not be shy about doing enough. Use the RPE as a guide for you. There are times when you want to see what you are made of. When you are struggling to sustain an RPE level for a particular exercise then it is time to move to the next exercise of your program. Choose 1 day/week or 1 day every other week where you take yourself to your limit. This effort will leave you gasping for air and – at the moment – wishing that you could stop, but don't. Make yourself proud and go for it.

Why is it important? The ability to sustain an effort is a statement that you are getting better. Getting better allows you to move to the next level.

How much duration do I need? Before you proceed to the next level, you should be proficient at your current level and able to sustain the effort. The goal is yours, and the schedule is yours. How quickly you proceed is based on your being able to safely endure your current effort.

You and your confidant should plan for success. Create a workout series that allows you to reach a stated goal. What is a stated goal? What should mine be?

A stated goal is just that. What do you want to achieve? You can have many, many fitness goals: increase stamina so that you can run a 10K without stopping, get your deadlift above 200 pounds or do a pull-up. Have all three of these goals! Get 50 more! It doesn't matter. These goals are yours and yours alone. Share them with your confidant and begin. Work and laugh with him/her as you prepare your approach. Be fully willing to change your approach as the plan unfolds. You'll do things that will not work. Laugh! It's a journey. Enjoy the ride. Every day is a beginning. Sure you'll build from yesterday. Sure yesterday won't matter. Sure yesterday was a waste. So what! Keep going!

When your workout begins you should "get into it." Make it fun and honestly want to do it. Many distractions will come your way. Understand that this is life, and there are times when the workout will have to step aside. This decision needs to be a conversation with yourself and needs to side with exercise. The priority should be your goals. Is this selfish? Could be. You're you. Your friends and family will benefit from your choice. You being healthier and fitter

161

will allow for many occasions to become special. This is worth your efforts. Be a role model in your circle.

A serious and often overlooked point that I feel necessary to make is that if you choose to "take some time off" you will lose considerable progress. A break should consist of no more than two consecutive days. More than that and you are at risk of sliding backwards which causes disappointments and many do the unthinkable – they quit. This is a real watch out for beginners.

Seldom does a workout need to be pushed aside and with the advent of 24/7 gyms, pushing them aside is usually only based on an excuse.

You should have short and long-term goals. In the short term, develop points along the way to achieve. Work to make these happen. Do not get in a hurry. Plan to succeed and make the success sustainable. Keep the long view.

I have a saying relating to exercise that I'm sure gets old – "If it doesn't matter, it doesn't matter!" What this means is that you should come away from an exercise effort with the feeling that you just outdid yourself. If the effort made you uncomfortable for a short period, good. Make it matter. You are worth it!

Form: What is it? Why is it important?

Form is a mode with which a repetition is completed. A correct form is the only one that should be used and the reason that it's important is safety. Form allows you to continue with your exercise program without injury.

Regardless of the maneuver, take the time to work on form first. Gain approval from a respected confidant on this particular motion. If it's an Olympic lift, ask someone you trust on Olympic lifts. If it's running, ask a qualified runner. If it's swimming, ask a qualified swimmer, etc. We're not all good at everything and should turn over our questions to actual experts of the discipline. We will want a single point source to answer all of our questions or we'll go to the internet for our answers. Do not do this. Ask for personal help regarding YOUR situation. You are important.

After the form has been analyzed and approved, begin the exploration process:

If you're doing cardio, mix it up. Start slow to make sure that your form sustains itself throughout. Then speed up, go longer, do intervals – whatever. Realize that you are the only one who knows what you feel like. Follow the advice that "If it doesn't matter, it doesn't matter." Basically, do not pursue junk exercise time.

If you're lifting weights, mix it up. Choose a mix of goals and try to reach ALL of them at the same time. This avenue of thought will force you to be comprehensive in your approach and to learn yourself. You'll "connect the dots" that your core affects deadlifts and your deadlifts will affect Power Cleans and squats which will affect your bench-press which affects the push press and on and on. If you and your confidant can come up with a solid set of goals and an approach to achieve them, you'll win. Remember that health is the ultimate goal of ALL exercise efforts.

The correct form on ALL moves is required to achieve success.

Understand that gains can only be made if you're not injured. Sound's very simple but one "oops" and you're out for a while and now have to go through the rigmarole of getting started again. This is not a small point as those of us who have gone through this can attest.

I've been injured and have had the opportunity to step back to where I used to be months ago. If you find yourself in this situation, start the process of accepting that you screwed up. Don't be too disappointed with yourself as you were just trying to get further than you had before. This is awesome but recognize that the faster you go, the more weight you try, the more repetitions that you're after only minimize the margin for error. Let me repeat that. The better you try to become the less room you have for error. Step back through your effort and find the mistake. Do not let any nuance go by – wrong is wrong. Use video to film yourself so you can find it. Don't miss this step and just go back to work. You HAVE to know what is wrong so you do not repeat.

This does not take away from the duration section above. Pushing yourself to your limit is important. Correct form is required for you to take yourself to your limit. You will not get hurt with good form and with good form, you will get better than even you thought you could!

Rest: What is it? Why is it important?

Rest is the tool we use to heal, revitalize, and refresh ourselves. Sleep – sounds simple – is the number one method to stay healthy; physically and mentally. Another important tool to rest is a day off. Plan these into your life and reap the rewards. We basically need eight hours of sleep per day and should take one day off per week so that our bodies stay fresh and can make continued gains.

Understand that rest is the period of the exercise process where improvements are actually made! The basic tenet of exercise is that we use exercise to tear ourselves up and then use rest to recover and get better.

Embrace the suck.

Your body is a very adaptable organism. When we exercise with intensity (RPE based), our body "freaks out" and muscles create micro-tears and we have soreness. This is very normal and more than "OK." When we eat properly and rest, we'll heal and adapt to this new challenge. Next time we encounter this level of intensity, we'll be ready for it! (This may not happen the first time, but it will happen and you will get better) Embrace this phenomenon. It's exciting to know that we're adaptable.

When we choose to not rest (as we are prone to do), we usually also will not assign our lack of gains to our lack of rest. This is really a simple concept. An unhealed micro-tear that is asked to repeat an exercise with the same intensity is still unhealed. A poor performance will occur and blame will start to be assigned – look at rest early on to see if you honestly gave that a chance.

It's perfectly OK to do other exercises and get a great workout in and achieve results – just rest the area of stress so that it adapts and can be ready for the next challenge.

If you can plan to work a muscle group – also plan to leave it alone. Be comprehensive so that you can reach your goals. Rest that group so that you can maximize your results.

Plan to take a day off. Plan is the key word – use your confidant at this point – talk to them and then listen. On your day off, do something that you enjoy – this doesn't equate to a "cheat day" in the context of eating all of the ice cream and pizza you want. A day off means to go for a hike, bike ride, swim, kayak, rock climb, etc. Enjoy your fitness. You've earned it and your body has earned it – enjoy it!

On the other side of the coin, understand that too much rest will lead to deterioration. Plan to get back to work. Keep the hammer down and get where you're going. You'll know what to do when you get there. I promise.

Longevity: What is it? Why is it important?

Longevity subscribes to the idea that you're never done. Getting there is important – keeping yourself there is more important. If you're doing the above – intensity, duration, form, and rest – you're on the right track. Don't come off tract. How do I do this?

Become a little bit defiant. Choose to dream of a next opportunity to "show off" your fitness. Complete a 5K and then plan for a next one. Go for a ½ marathon and then plan for a next one. Obstacle Course Racing (OCR) – choose one and then choose a next one. Getting bored with your current choices – OK – choose a different genre. Make it harder – increase your satisfaction and don't stop. Announce your next event on social media. Once you've signed up, bring it to everyone's attention that you're a beast. The positive feedback you will receive will be an inspiration to continue.

Choose to get better at what you've chosen. Get better at the 5K, ½ marathon, OCR, etc. Make it a game for you to improve. Find a way to get inspired – books, movies, internet searches. Learn of your deficiency and then learn to better it. It's fun, and you'll become a better you. Don't become satisfied. Mix it up. Kayak, run, hike, bike, OCR, skydive, snorkel, scuba dive, water ski, snow ski, etc. You are your own boss – find an interest and then explore it. Your own common sense will dictate the depth of your involvement. Worried about money? Don't! As you get healthier, your expenses will go down and as you get healthier, your existing bad habits will cease and that will help fund these opportunities. Circle back. As you explore new exciting adventures and distance yourself from your current ones, there will come a time when you should revisit the current ones to see if you're as good as you thought you were. You might be better. You might not. Who knows until you try? In between events, practice to get better. You'll be surprised at what you will learn. I personally plan for the next year's event schedule in January of the New Year. I sign up right away and then get to work to make each event the best that I can make it. I purposefully choose events that are "incredible" in my mind. 150-mile bike ride, marathon, ½ marathon, and Off Course Race, etc. I can only do a few of these per year but each one is an enormous challenge unto themselves. These events do a great job keeping me in check and focused.

The key is to keep going. Never stop > never be satisfied > never worry about failure. Keep the train going!

Fun: What is it? How do I make exercise fun? Why is it important?

I know that you know what fun is. It's what you enjoy doing, right? You need to enjoy and have fun with exercise!

There are many cases that I see where a customer comes to the gym to lose weight and treat it like a punishment for their bad living. This group wants to do as little as possible and get the maximum results.

This approach leads to failure. Life is a choice – choose to enjoy exercise. Note that you will be wrong multiple times – the workout, the people, etc., may suck. Equipment that you were counting on isn't available or out of order – sucks. You need to accept these as temporary let downs and move forward. Tomorrow will happen and you will get another opportunity. Basically, don't worry about it. Come to your workout with the goal of getting better and to have fun. In the world of self-improvement, we need to accept that we have to spend time on self-social engineering and that we have to do this in a dynamic and conscious way.

What do I do?

All six components of exercise NEED to be incorporated in your creation. Sit back with your confidant and seriously discuss this topic. By all means, be selfish and creative. The weight of each component can change and you should know who you really are with respect to this effort. If you are a novice and find that the only goal that comes to mind for you is weight loss then place fun at the top of YOUR priority list. Hopefully your confidant will divert your weight loss goal to a deeper one that will give you life-long satisfaction. Weight loss will come on its own. You do not have to worry about that. Focus on making exercise fun!

If you are a driven athlete, then intensity and duration may be YOUR priority. Fun is still required but elsewhere on your list.

Getting older. Longevity may be YOUR priority. Fun is still required but elsewhere on your list.

Start where you are. This is why the development needs to include your confidant and be dynamic. Basically, you probably don't know how to weight these components and it will change anyway. Re-evaluate constantly and learn to roll with it. Assign the six components of exercise their appropriate weight in YOUR priorities.

Change it up – what is fun today may be mundane tomorrow. Do scheduled "gut" checks to make sure that you are satisfied with your approach. Routine can be the enemy. Seek an approach that allows flexibility. Use your confidant frequently and be honest.

Get into a group – the more the better. While having a partner help you on your journey is great, there are periods of time when that partner has reasons to not be available for you and vice versa. A larger group has the same issue but enough people allowing someone from the group to be there to help motivate you. Sign up for an event of your choosing. Exercising with an event in mind gives purpose to the effort as you are working to achieve a goal. This excitement is added motivation and will keep you moving. You may have events where others will come with you and times where you will do the event alone. It's all good.

Mix it up. I have participated in events including running, bicycling, obstacle course racing, hiking, trail running, etc. I follow the "Jack of All Trades, Master of None" approach to fitness. Be a generalist so that you can experience any event that catches your fancy.

Plan your calendar in advance – I spend the late fall and winter determining what my next year's event calendar will look like. After all the determination and decisions, I book the events as soon as they become available. This booking has many benefits as the event itself is cheaper, travel is available, lodging is available, I'm committed, I now have a plan, my stress is less as the schedule is now determined, and I can just work the new year to my advantage. Awesome!

The importance of fun cannot be overstated. The other five components of exercise are directly tied to this. Intensity, duration, form, rest, longevity all have ties to fun. If you enjoy what you are doing, you will continue doing it. Embrace your need to enjoy your life. It's beyond OK to enjoy your life.

On another note: What if you have been going down the wrong road for a long time? You agree with all that has been written but why should I believe this stuff. The whole industry has told me to buy this or buy that. I'm fat and have little motivation. This game is not fun any longer. I'm over it!

While I agree with your anger, get over it. Time waits for no one.

The real answer is that I am sorry and you are where you are. Begin the right way right now. Any widget that is being promoted as YOUR ANSWER is very likely not. Hard, intense, and smart work is required for your success. I cannot emphasize enough that your confidant needs to have drunk this Kool-Aid. Tomorrow, you will be one day older than today. Do not hesitate to get on the right approach. Be thoughtful and be successful!

What if I do nothing? Can I stay where I am at?

I am being honest here. This is what most people believe and want. The feeling that we are destined to have ailments is rampant. The feeling that our genetics plays an undeniable role in our future is rampant. The feeling that the process of aging is all downhill, is rampant. What is the point of exercising and trying? I will just stay where I am and deal with what comes to me. Why not?

The reality is that none of the rampant feelings are entirely wrong. You will have ailments, get old, your genetics will play a role in your future. Again, I am sorry. Nothing I can say or do will take these 100% away.

What I can say with confidence is that doing nothing will exasperate the issues. I had a co-worker who used to tell me frequently that "nothing is ever so bad that it cannot get worse." He is right and this phrase is applicable. Doing nothing will make your future worse. Worse in the way of expense – you will pay much more for healthcare and worse in the quality of life you can expect.

If you do nothing, can you stay where you are at? Not a chance! We are held together through maintenance. We have to take care of ourselves daily. We brush our teeth, shower, use deodorant, eat, etc. daily and barely consider this an effort. If we do not eat, do not brush our teeth, do not clean up – things will go bad. We will not be in the same place. Exercising should be viewed in the same light. If we do not exercise – things will go bad. We will not be in the same place.

Kids: What approach should you take with your kids?

This is always a tricky question and it also is a "per child" answer. In other words, no one answer will be applicable to all kids. There is, however, a basic premise that should be instilled in all youth. Exercise needs to be a part of your life and that is all. Exercise needs to be viewed by kids as basic as brushing their teeth is. In the world of kids, fun holds higher sway and this is where the focus needs to be placed. Find out what your kids like to do that is active and then mindfully pursue it.

Ball sports are great and a lot can be learned from them. Teamwork, leadership, competitiveness, etc. are all components of ball sports. Awesome if your kids like this then the availability for them is usually easy. This way you have coaches who can help your child succeed. The role of the parent is tricky. What I mean by this is that team sports have an inherent danger built into them. Participants tend to love the atmosphere and crave the camaraderie, which is great, I am glad for this opportunity.

There are two issues though and the first is the biggest. This involves the reality that the team will not be together at some point and usually while the participant is still young. The child will get cut, graduation will separate the participants, folks will move, the season will be over, etc. Anything can and will happen. Even if the person plays into their middle years – at some point the game will be over. And here is the question – Then what? This moment usually leads to the need to "take a break." Which is code for "I don't know what to do now so I'll do nothing and claim to be taking a break"; "no one will say anything negative about getting back on a horse and might even say that I deserve a break." Do you remember earlier in the chapter where I said that people would come to the gym to "relive their glory days"? This is why. It's hard to keep team sports going through your golden years. Plan to transition into individual sports so that YOU succeed. This is hard to do but the sooner the better.

The next issue is a subpart of the first one. One of the goals of a team sport is for the team to get better. What is lost in this is the idea that the child needs to get better by themselves and then apply this success to the team. This is not an easy task and requires the development of a skill that transfers to the sport and also develops an enduring love of fitness for the kid. While this may sound easy, it's not. Learning to throw/catch a football/baseball or shoot/dribble a basketball is essential within these sports but hardly applicable to life off of the field or court. The coach may be happy with the progression but the future use of the newly found skill will be lacking. Discover and implement the importance of personal fitness development. Keep it enjoyable and make it a natural part of your life.

Individual sports that the youth loves is awesome. Let the kid develop this love and foster growth so that kid's future contains this sport at a responsible level. And what I mean by a responsible level is that while I loved to run, I knew that I was not going to the Olympics. I, therefore, kept running and was satisfied with the results that I achieved. Of course, I wanted to be better but also I knew the Olympics were out of my league. I was fine with that but could easily participate through local 5Ks, ½ marathons, marathons, and now I can easily participate with bicycling and Off Course Racing. I can easily practice on my own or with friends. I'm in charge and love it.

Conclusion: This chapter is designed to help you to understand and help yourself. Granted it's not a "how to" chapter (nor is it intended to be) as it leaves practically all of the details up to you to decide. I sincerely hope that you accept that you are the boss of you. This effort is about you making you a better you. Not an easy task but you're worth all of it. The time to start is now.

Regarding your kids – get them on their journey early and promote satisfactory growth that relates to them as an individual. A lifelong love affair with getting better physically will lead to many other opportunities and successes.

Chapter Ten
Motivation

Motivation is a real key to success. Becoming healthy is a great aspiration but it also requires the answer to "Why?"

Getting to your grassroots answer is very important and seldom as easy as it sounds.

As a fitness center owner, what I hear most is, what I term as, mirror related. The goal of losing weight, getting toner, losing that flab underneath your arms, getting back to high school days of glory, etc. What I want to tell people is that these types of goals need to be side effects of becoming fit and not the goal of becoming fit. We need to realize that we have spent far too long on the wrong health path. We have yo-yo dieted, drifted in and out of gyms, done nothing, started or are growing a family, married, divorced, adopted, career managed, ate badly, drank too much, slept too little, etc. And we wonder why we are in a mess.

Then, to fix these nightmarish behaviors, we look at the mirror and want to "look" better. I'm hoping that you can see the scope of the dichotomy presented here. Serious issues are not conquered by rigging the body to "look" better.

I am aware that we want an easy solution to our problems, and that we want this solution to be fast, cheap, and easy. You know – the proverbial magic pill. You also know – the one that doesn't exist. My advice is to spend zero time lying to yourself. If you have identified with any of the bad behaviors listed, or you have your own list, then you know what you need to deal with. I am also here to tell you that you cannot buy your solution because you need to be your solution. There are no pills, supplements, home equipment that you can buy to get you where you need to go. Now, there will be money involved but it's to facilitate your success and not create it. Basically, it's your body and mind so you need to do the work to get the benefits. The breakthrough for you to do is to fully accept your role in success. You're worth it. Now do it!

What other factors are quality motivators? There are always many possibilities for this answer, and I encourage you to search honestly for your reasoning. I will touch on a few other high-level reasons to get your brain working, but I am fully aware that your reason is yours. Be real and look beyond the mirror.

Economics

This is a reason that intertwines with all you do. With fitness: The basic question to ask yourself is: Is it cheaper to be healthy or to be unhealthy? This a question that I will bet that you get the right answer 100% of the time. It's obvious. Being healthy costs less! For every one dollar we invest in wellness, we get six dollars in return. That's a 600% return on investment. Remember, we're thrilled with seven percent in the stock market. We all know that healthy makes better sense, right? Great. You're on board! Now what do we actually do?

What I am told on a frequent basis is that people would eat healthy if it didn't cost so much. As if eating crap is cheap. Fast food is cheap? Soda is cheap? Healthy food is very inexpensive when we figure in the added cost of cancer, diabetes, heart disease, high blood pressure and the like. Also, what I have found is that healthy food costs less than the cheap stuff when you do it yourself. Using only raw ingredients from a good grocery store and/or a farmer's market and making the food yourself puts you in touch with what you put in your mouth. I would bet that you are a lot pickier than a fast food worker or a food processor. You do have to provide a little brainpower and be willing to trip over your own feet a time or two to come up with the quality and convenience that you need. Start with what you know is a winner. We understand that your taste buds matter, so satisfy them. Go to the spice aisle and try. Determine what makes you happy and repeat it. Then, go to the next item, become successful, and then repeat again. This won't take too long and you will have a huge menu to choose from. A very economical and huge menu.

Another large factor in the consideration of health is the cost of exercise. We're not going to get overly dramatic on this. Until you get an excellent confidant, choose the correct answer. This is a dead-on statement: Stay away from the cheap gyms. If you are debating on your sincerity regarding healthy living, little will dis-incentivize more than an unwelcoming place pretending to be a fitness center. You won't know what to do and you'll walk on the treadmill.

Oooh. There is little opportunity that you will come out a winner. Please understand that more people fail at becoming healthy than succeed. By joining a cheap gym, you diminish your odds of success too much to risk it. The advice is to shop for results and then choose a location where you fit. Take the trial offer and make sure but make the choice based on your health success and not price. Make your goals your priorities! Remember: One dollar in gets you a 600% return. This is an economic opportunity that is huge, but it does take some honest effort on your part. You're all proud of that three percent pay increase. Wouldn't you like a 600% pay increase?

Don't get caught up in fashion regarding exercise either. You do not know what you need until you get involved. Comfort will definitely get you started and you will learn what functions are important when you want to step it up. Jumping to the answer too early often leads to an embarrassing admission that you do not know what you are doing. Just wait until you understand your needs. Cheaper in the short and long term.

Supplements: Forget them. Eat real food. Save your money and live better. Basically, you will never need a supplement. They are usually very poor quality, always overpriced, and you can get more usable nutrients from real food. I am, however, in favor of the high-quality nutrition bars and gel packs out there. There are several fitness-minded providers out there who work to really help you succeed. Use them as needed.

Family

Your family should always come first. What better way to honor your commitment to them than to be healthy and fit. Your spouse, children, parents, cousins, etc., all benefit from seeing their crazy family member care about themselves to the point of ridicule and not worrying about it. This type of motivation cuts both ways in that you are motivated by knowing that your activities are being chronicled, and they are being motivated by seeing your involvement and happiness.

Children always carry an extra special place in our hearts. We truly want them to succeed. Our approach to health and fitness as examples of how to live sends a powerful message to our young ones that self-sufficiency, self-motivation, problem solving, life-loving, active, caring, etc., is what should happen, and that we want that for them. Get them involved and make their health and fitness important too!

Families also extend to neighbors, co-workers, club members, etc. as well. The more that you are out there trying, the more positive feedback you will receive and even your, not so good performances will be celebrated as long as you power forward and get on to the next opportunity. People will try to emulate your path and/or cut their own path. Use the adage that "imitation is the greatest form of flattery" and be proud. You are their leader and they are following you.

On the other hand, if you are not active and are looking to be, what better honor can you give a friend or relative than to join in their activity or to have your own and share stories with them? Having a common point to discuss can take any family activity to another level of enjoyment. You might even be too busy talking to eat and not even know you missed it. Many families get together and have little to say. This puts an end to that!

Your Health and Fitness

Little doubt that many people begin this journey as a result of a realization that they aren't where they want to be at this point in their life and want to do something about it. As a gym owner, I see this every day and want to offer some serious advice. Are you ready? Make damn sure you have fun during your transition. Many want to start slow and work themselves into it. This approach has a high rate of failure as results do not come and frustration and boredom set in. Excuses for not attempting become the norm and quitting the only real option. Then we will see you in January for you to do it all over again. Do not choose this. Having fun and focusing on having more fun lets you forget about your problems and then they proceed to go away. Fun is too huge to dismiss or to marginalize.

Another axiom that we struggle watching is "Something is better than nothing." No it's not. It's the same thing. Nothing. Use this axiom instead: "If it doesn't matter, it doesn't matter." Your success depends on your effort. A little effort yields a little result and very frequently results in frustration – leading to the feeling of failure – and ultimately, quitting.

Instead, choose an event that will challenge you to climb into the new you. Your health and fitness will improve without your focusing on it. You do not need to do that. Choose the event. Have a goal. Make it aggressive for you, and then make that happen. And for crying out loud – have fun! Be serious about your success. Do not let diversions get in your way. Remember that you are the one with the aforementioned realization of bad health. Right?

A very large component of your health and fitness is to take the time to become educated on nutrition and then use this advice. If it is not simple and uses real ingredients that you assemble – leave it on the shelf. What is important to realize about the group that has wavered to their current status of health is that you have made many, many poor choices.

A huge understanding for you is that simple solutions cuts two ways. To eat like you're currently eating and then just add "magic" supplements or to use "magic" supplements and decrease your crappy eating (but still eat crap), is a bad move. The other simple (the better one) involves some brainpower on your behalf and a little planning. Understand this: Whole food, real food, simple preparations is simple too. The difference is that the results are way better. Get used to preparation. Don't make a big deal of it, but do it. This isn't a chore. It's your life.

Remember that you are choosing this motivation due to poor choices in the past. The key words of the last sentence are "in the past." Work forward. Choose to enjoy your journey and never tire of getting better. Plateaus may happen down the road, but don't worry about that until you reach one. Who cares? Get to work and get through it.

The Benefits

Having long-term benefits as your motivation is rewarding but so is enjoying the ride there. The benefits of a healthy lifestyle that are real and reliable include stress reduction, better sleep, control over your day (this is your time), better mobility, higher energy, less illness, weight control, additional friend group, lower cost living, etc. Being able to choose a self-improvement project that yields these kinds of rewards is special. All the rewards listed have merit and are tangible and the beautiful part is that they are available to 100% of you. They are quick to happen and get better over time.

Let's expand on a couple of these benefits and clean up some misconceptions.

Higher Energy: What we hear is "How does this make sense? You just ran 3 miles. How can you have more energy? Aren't you tired?" The reality is: Nope! I've never felt better and more alive than after accomplishing this run. Your body appreciates the task given to it and responds with an increase of energy. We need to understand that our bodies are made to move. What makes us "tired" is sitting, laying, and doing nothing. We're made to move and we react positively when we do.

Lower cost of living: What we hear is "How is this possible? You eat healthy food and pay to exercise. Doesn't that cost a lot?" The reality is: Nope! Eating healthy and exercising keeps me healthy and, therefore, out of the doctor's office. I never miss work and am reliable as an employee. I'm higher energy than my co-workers, so I get the better job opportunities and higher pay. So, lower cost and higher pay. Win!

Additional friend group: When you choose to be healthy by eating right and exercising, you will not be alone. Like-minded people seek each other out so they can share advice and to have a "buddy" to do what you like. These people will likely be new to you and yet they're awesome and will help any way they can. Look to them for inspiration and be inspirational yourself. Awesome on all fronts!

Better sleep: Didn't we say earlier that you'd have higher energy? Yep, but when you are ready to bed down and sleep, your body will seek renewal and not just rest. Your sleep will be deeper as a result and be better rested. Again-another win for you.

Having a healthy approach to life and experiencing these benefits is not difficult. You will receive them and be happier in the process. One advice that we'd recommend is to be aware of the benefits when you get them and realize where they came from. We've seen people work to get healthy and, actually receive these benefits, then they forget where they came from and just assume that they happen regardless of what they do. Not true. As soon as you cease living a healthy lifestyle, your benefits go away as well. Like gravity: You can go upward forever as long as you keep going. If you ease up, you'll quickly come back down to where you started.

Kids – What motivates them? Your assistance needed.

Kids are an exciting and different adventure as they come in all ages, shapes, sizes, and interests but motivation needs to be instilled into them from you. Be healthy and here's how. Teach your kids that if they're healthy and fit, they will be viewed as a more desirable candidates for work, college, etc. As parents, we need to start early in their developmental stages to instill solid values in them. Make sure they see you trying. Immediate success may not be overly important, but consistent effort is. Take them to events that you participate in and let them be engaged with likeminded people so they learn to appreciate their self-worth and self-responsibility. What I want to emphasize is the concept of self-responsibility. While having an active child in sports or clubs is important, so is the idea that they need to be in charge of themselves regarding their physical and mental development. You should guide them and give them the tools but they need to want and do this for themselves. In ten to twenty years when they are completely independent, they need to have the desire to be self-motivated and to maintain their fitness level.

Here is where things can get off track and what you should do about it. When the opportunity comes for your child to participate in sports, the likelihood that the sport is team based is very high. Softball, soccer, basketball, football are very popular. They should be. They teach teamwork, participation, leadership, etc. Awesome! And we believe in these activities. The motivation for these groupings comes from the camaraderie of the teammates and coaches and will carry the kid until they are either no longer interested in this sport, they're hurt or aren't good enough to continue. The reality is that something will stop this activity. This fact is why parent need to instill into their child the inner love of health and fitness so that when the glory days become a thing of the past, the child can go

184

forward on their own. Many people come to my gym wanting desperately to relive their "glory" days. I'm sorry, but they are gone.

What does a parent do? When the opportunities begin to present themselves for T-ball, dancing, football, soccer, whatever – embrace them – openly and fully. They're awesome and help you to instill very good values. In conjunction, and this is fun too, take your kid to do individual activities as well. Swimming, hiking, bicycling, skateboarding, rock climbing, etc. These opportunities are cheap and fun for everyone and instill values that are somewhat similar with the team-based activities but also show the child that their individual development is appreciated and valued. If they get better or not is not as relevant as seeing that an honest interest is explored and enjoyed. This way – when the team-based activities cease (and they will) – the child has an easy transition into forever activities. These are all positive additions to your child's life and will keep a fire burning long after the spotlight shuts off.

Conclusion

Motivation is probably the deepest factor towards your approach and success with becoming health and fitness minded. Accepting that your ball is in your own court is paramount to a long-term approach. Understanding that you do not need to fully develop what motivates you prior to beginning your journey is beyond OK. Likewise, not having a vanity-based motivation ever is also – beyond OK. Whatever motivates you to improve and maintain your health and fitness needs to be based on honesty and not vanity.

The examples that I have listed: family, kids, you, economics, benefits are just that – examples. You may choose from these individually or it could be a combination of these along with some of your own. Only you should care. It's your body and your life. By keeping it healthy and fit, you will be able to fully participate in the lives of those around you. Your cost of living will be surprisingly low and your energy level surprisingly high. You will not be sick, your attention span will be better, you won't miss work and will likely be rewarded for being a good employee. There are so many benefits that it is impossible to name all of them.

What is important for you to do is to get going. Not having all your ducks in a row is OK. Hesitating because of it is not. Keeping your goals away from vanity or trying to relive your past is necessary as people get stuck with these two and try to begin slow and then ease into their "routine." The need to hit a vanity target isn't there. What's the big deal? You're not skinny now and everyone accepts you the way you are so there's no hurry to change. Right? Same with trying to relive your past. There's no hurry to accomplish that either is there? The right choice is to choose a goal that is meaningful and hard for you to achieve. Now do what you need to do to accomplish this. If you sign up for a 5K in three months, you've got three months to get ready. If you've signed up for an off-course race in six months and it's a couple of states away, you've got six months to get ready. You've got to get your travel organized, vacation time requested, etc. You've got stuff to do, and you had better get at it. Spend the money and commit. The activity it triggers will purely assist you to get ready to succeed and then...guess what? You'll get healthy and fit in the process. Awesome!

What's Stopping You?

This is a counter question to what is motivating you. If you were to ask everyone today if they could improve their health and fitness through nutrition and exercise, you would receive a 100% "Sure would!" So where is everyone? What is stopping you?

Many people are believing in an all or nothing strategy. We simply believe that there is not a middle ground and vanity is the reason anyway. Or "I'll get to it later." Blah, blah, blah. "In January, I'll stop eating and go to the gym five nights a week and will look like a model in days and it'll be awesome!" Slow down. Won't happen that way.

When we present people's plan for improvement as stated above, they laugh and mock the ideas. Who would ever do this? We agree with this mockery. However, this is what many, many people actually do. The urge to find a fast solution to years of poor choices is high. We need to accept that the magic pill does not exist! If we would just be diligent for six lousy months, 80% of our wishes would come true. I realize that diligence for six months is hard. I really do. Temptations will not go away so we need to say no to them. I understand that showing weakness is not considered OK, but the reality is that we are weak. That is why we are in the shape that we are in. If we were to show you in a moment by moment reality of what we're doing,

187

we'd fix this easily. The reality is that we don't manage moment by moment. We believe that this moment may be poorly done but the next moment will be better. Then we do it again. Stop it! Each moment counts. Each and every one of them.

Some of the disincentive involves the souring from our constant efforts not working out for us. We believe, mistakenly, that we are different and that our genetics will not allow us to be healthy and that it is OK as the medical community will help us when it is needed. Our genetics are not much different than they were over a million years ago. What is different in this day and age is to have choices that allow us to be "happy" for a moment and perpetually forgo our health and fitness in the search of another "happy" moment. After a while, time goes by, and we find ourselves in horrible shape. Then we go back to blaming our genetics. Nope. We just gave in to marketing and are suffering for it. Both economically and physically. A question that always appears on forms at medical offices involve family history. (Therefore, perpetuating the idea of genetics being the cause of our ailment.) The questions are usually, "Does heart disease, diabetes, cancer, etc. run in your family?" If you say yes, the physician will ask you about it and so the conversation goes. What should happen in questioning any of the yeses should be regarding the lifestyles of the family. Did they also smoke, eat crap, and didn't exercise effectively? How about questioning the lifestyle of the patient? Do you smoke? Eat and drink crap? Exercise? How many problems could be prevented with a serious approach to personal health and fitness?

Also, our constantly failing efforts are creating a stigma on us and we are afraid to try again. We will look foolish so why try? The simple answer is YOU MATTER! While I understand your point regarding failure, please understand the definition of insanity. If you keep doing the same thing over and over again, yet expect different results – good luck. Take a thoughtful approach, talk with several professionals whom you believe and respect. Merge the ideas and create a plan for yourself or better yet, let someone lead you. The point is: This time be thoughtful and have a plan that you know will work. It has to include a serious reasonableness factor which takes into consideration what you will actually do. If you know this is a "pie in the sky" approach – stop. I do not believe that you want to waste your time anymore. I truly want you to make an effort but I sincerely hope that you can better understand my comment that 'something is better than nothing' is silly as they are the same thing. Basically, be thoughtful and then be successful.

"We don't have time" is another reason for not taking care of ourselves. I'm believing that another way to say this is that we have too much stress in our lives and if we remove preventative care from our schedule that we will be more flexible with our time and able to better handle our busyness. Another line of thinking is "It won't work anyway." We really need to get over these thought processes and truly believe that YOU MATTER. You should not try to escape this point. I understand that your kids, parents, co-workers, spouse, etc. are important. They are. So are you. With the advent of the 24/7 gyms and easy communication, some planning and nutritional management, you can accomplish anything at any time. To say that you don't have time needs thought about. You are too important and your benefits completely outweigh the inconvenience. Why would you not?

"I'm too old to start this stuff." Personally, I'm 57 years old and have yet to consider age as a deterrent on any front. There is little truer than the knowledge that the older we get the more concerned about healthy living we should be. Aging is usually not good for us and in order to alleviate the aches and pains and to keep mobile, we have to pursue as vigorous a routine that we can muster. The first step is to know where you are physically and make an appropriate plan to succeed. This is very much a case where you should get with several smart fitness buffs and collectively generate an assessment of your skills and then plan accordingly. Negating or reversing the aging process to the best of your ability is very much worth the effort. Understand that you can improve at any age, and you should do – all you can – while you can. The difference between doing all you can and sitting on the couch means either dancing at age eight , visiting your family (you drive), mowing your own yard, living in your house or watching TV at eighty and having your license taken away as you're not safe on the road anymore and then getting moved into a nursing home. This is a real choice and the chooser is you.

Another thing that's stopping you: "My significant other told me not to." Yep. This happens. A lot. In person, I would have to stay out of your business as it's none of mine, but in a book I'm free from that burden. To me, there are three possibilities for that type of behavior – none of which succeed. The first and best explanation is that they are worried that you will get hurt. This is an honest concern as they may have seen/heard of instances where exercise created a situation that went bad and a person got hurt. This is extremely rare, but it can happen. What you should do is show them that you are serious and have a serious plan that takes into consideration all the concerns with personal safety ranking high on the list of priorities. Take into consideration all their legitimate concerns and show the resolution to them. Co-planning may yield a better result and that is awesome in and of itself.

"We might get hurt." Some feel that it is a commonly known fact that those who exercise are likely to experience injuries, and you don't want to be one of them. Let me be clear. Any physical activity creates a chance for injury. Let me also be clear. Sitting on the couch and doing nothing will create lethargy and ultimately illnesses that do not get better the longer you sit. Be smart and go to smart people. Knowing what to do by yourself is going to be difficult out of the gate. We should not even try to do this without caring and knowledgeable people around us. On our own, we can under-eat or over-eat. We can lift too much or too little. Our form can be bad and cause injury or be ineffective. To be worried about being hurt is actually pretty healthy. Use this worry in a positive way and make sure that the infrastructure around you is solid. Now is not the time to be shy and think about "little ol'me" not worth worrying about, etc. BS – YOU MATTER. Be concerned and find quality assistance. If the first person you ask doesn't impress you, look for the second, third, whatever. The importance of your effort and success cannot be overstated.

The second related concern is they do not want you to fail. They know that you have tried in the past and do not want you to get hurt. This has merit and very nice and puts the burden on you to ensure that your plan is thought out and solid. You should present your plan to this person and go through with it. You both can learn from this, and with proper presentation, you might just get yourself a solid workout partner. An issue with workout partners is that they may become future boat anchors. Best intentions are often temporary and you do not want this. So avoid being reliant upon a workout partner. YOU MATTER. Let nothing get in your way.

The third potential is the one that I like the least but I know that it does exist. There are people who will want to control you, and you cannot let them. The "I love you just the way you are" crap needs to go by the wayside. YOU MATTER. It's as simple as that. If you feel that you are being bullied, be straightforward and direct. You can try the nice stuff but be clear. You are doing this and will not tolerate theatrical nonsense nor any manipulation. Stick to your guns on this and be prepared for any shenanigans. You do not deserve them so do not accept them. You deserve support and should get it. Be firm and be direct.

While there are many "reasons" to not become healthy minded, few of them matter. Do the right thing and get going. Make and execute a plan for your success.

An unfortunate de-motivator for people is the realization that they are not in the shape they thought they would be in at this point in their life. I've had many folks come to me who are emotionally tied to their high school sports career. I try to remind them to begin where they currently are and to realize that their high school years are behind them and forever will be. Many of these folks will also be "sure" that they know how to exercise and then proceed to grossly underdo or grossly overdo their workout. Either approach leads directly to short-term efforts and poor results. The concept that their health is a journey and not a destination needs to be accepted. This is basically a hare versus turtle scenario where the rabbit may be faster out of the gate but the turtle uses the slow and steady approach and wins the race. Being patient for the outward benefits of weight loss is a little harder but do not get hung up on vanity goals as they are a death nail to your fitness. Way less than one percent of us are models. We do not need vanity goals! Be the turtle. The results are real and worth it.

Some of the concern for this group of reminiscers is they view their fitness resurgence as a chore and want to "bang it out and get back to their glory days." They tend to purposefully omit fun from their approach as "they are serious this time." Why? You are not at work. This is your time. Please have as much fun as you can. Fun will help you through your rough patches where results are slower than you'd prefer. Whatever you do, bake as much fun into your day as you can. You are worth it! Have a good time and enjoy life. The worst-case scenario for having fun is that you may slightly slow down your progress, but I guarantee you – those who enjoy what they are doing will do it longer. Again – be the turtle.

A similar concern is that you will not be good at stuff you try. Yeah? And? Who knew that? Others may point out your deficiencies. Really? Guess what – the rest of everyone else sucks too. Get over yourself and have fun. This is an issue that I see far too often. Remember that your goal is not vanity nor looking good to others. Your goal is to be healthy, have fun and know that the vanity stuff will happen as you progress.

I want to spend a moment on these two topics as the power they render is dramatic and gives insecurity to many people. We give far too much strength to imaginary people. We want results and we want them now. And we want them to last. None of these beliefs are healthy. To say that we don't have these beliefs, though, would be very misleading. Humans have a lot of pride and do not want to appear that we do not know what we are doing nor do we want to believe that we are not in complete charge of ourselves. I'm not sure where or when we got overly confident about ourselves but it does happen. (I would speculate that as we graduate high school that we feel like we need to look like we have it all under control.) And it is very damaging to our psyche. We honestly know things aren't right but we have other obligations (work and family seem to take the top spots). We start seeking excuses for our physical result. We do not like where we are but it's OK. We think we can fix it quickly. It doesn't matter. People will look at us funny, etc. You know – anything other than actually taking corrective action. I will not deny that the recognition of where we are is hurtful to our pride but we need to accept this reality and get the plan together to combat the issue for the long term.

Along with this same logic is – we do not want to be selfish. No one wants to be labelled selfish as this has a bad connotation and deservingly so. The question from me is – which is more selfish – taking the time to take care of yourself or not? Any time that you spend on yourself away from your work or family is selfish – right? Nope. Not taking care of yourself will lead you to be a high maintenance person who needs frequent doctor visits, more medicines, more sleep, more money for this stuff, etc. There are one hundred sixty-eight hours in a week. Spend two and a half of them on yourself, and you will discover more energy and time for everyone and everything else. You will be far from selfish if you can do more with your awake hours and being fit will help you accomplish this.

When your health is on the line, it is very valuable to be honest with yourself. You only get one you. Take care of yourself as no one else can. Getting out of your own way is hard but necessary. The older that I get the more I understand that many, many people are better than me and I'll never catch them. The chance that I may become the best at something is over with. Get OK with that paradigm. You're going to face it. We will never be as good as we once were. You can reminisce if you want to but a return to your glory days may not happen and you need to be OK with this. This is why many events have age groups. We can compete with our peers and not with everyone. Events are even sorted by gender (And the reality is: you don't have to compete at all.) Just do it as a social gathering. Meet like-minded people or to just have fun.

Maybe you have given up? Your health is bad. You're overweight. You smoke. You drink. You've not exercised in years. You're old. What's the point? etc. Talk about a list of de-motivators. Wow! What should this group do? This group needs to accept that YOU MATTER and truly take it to heart. This group needs a professional fitness expert right away to guide them. Missteps for this group can be devastating. Get over yourself and let someone help you.

You are never too late, but major changes are needed in your attitude, direction, and effort.

"I don't have the money. I can barely afford to eat." Understand that becoming healthy requires an investment to get there. Look at your expenses and see where you can come up with the funds to make this one. Of all the investments out there – stocks, bonds, homes, whatever – you being healthy is the most fruitful one. Getting seven percent return on an investment is considered good. Spending $400-$500 on your health can easily save you $20,000 in medical treatments. Type 2 diabetics generally costs someone around that much per year. I doubt that congestive heart failure or COPD are cheaper. Plus being healthy can put you in a position to get a better job and you can say "Yes!" to opportunities as they arise. I understand that some money is required up front and that you may not immediately have it. Do yourself a favor though. Look at your expenses and find the money. If you eat out at all during the month, you can probably scrounge up the needed money to get you on the right track. Get the money. Get going and make sure that you have the help you need to succeed. Just spending money is not enough. You need to purchase a result. Put the infrastructure in place to accomplish this and ask for professional help to know what the infrastructure looks like. Do not assume that you know what is needed (If you knew, you would have done it by now.)

Kids. It's a little harder to understand why they are not on the healthy bandwagon. I'll have to break it to you – this is a parent's responsibility. Instilling a healthy mindset into your children should be just as important as honesty and good manners. There isn't much more important than the responsibility to be a great parent. But – let's be real – as we look out the window, we see kids everywhere who are diabetic, stare at their phones, stuck in some game, non-active, overweight, etc. None of this is OK. What do we do? We need to reverse this outcome.

Begin before they are born. Eating healthy and exercising for both mom and dad prior to birth makes it easier to instill healthy values going forward. You're basically getting a positive running start at the right thing. Show your growing baby the casual importance of eating healthy and being active and they simply won't know any different. The awesomeness here is that a sincere start like this will make the next 18+ years easier for you. They will probably be on you to live better before you know it!

If you've missed your early opportunity to set a great precedence, and you've done the first fast food excursion or birthday parties with cake and ice cream and/or discovered the wonderful screens, what do you do? How do you get them away from this? (You need away from it too.) Here is a great reality: Kids are very understanding and forgiving. They want to please you, and if you say that you made a mistake, they will be OK with changing (as long as you do.) Use the "oops" moment to strengthen your bond and hold each other accountable. They help you and you help them. Win – Win! You are not a bad parent by changing away from terrible products and this is a good opportunity to display the changing times. Understand that type 2 diabetes used to be called Adult Onset Diabetes. Kids seldom were type 2. That is no longer true. Kids are increasingly diagnosed with type 2 diabetes, and it is completely unnecessary. Parents have the obligation to love and care for their child. No parent wants their kid to get or be sick, so why do we give them soda, watch screens, prevent activity, and expect that bad won't happen? Peel these negatives away! Set limits and hold to them. You are the parent and are responsible for their path to adulthood. Being healthy going into adulthood is a great stepping-stone to a happy and exciting life. You have the opportunity and the obligation to make this happen.

Your kids are early teenagers and have great habits. They're driven, motivated and doing great. What do you do? First off, enjoy this! You've done a great job and are now reaping the results of your efforts. See if you can enhance them in anyway. Ask them. Keep a distant eye on them to make sure they stay on track. (They probably will but you should watch to make sure.) Also, see if you can learn from them. I bet they are great teachers and can help you be the best you can be too! What a compliment to both of you to have them teach you! That would be great.

And now the hard one. Your kids are early teenagers and have bad habits galore. What do you do? You are the adult responsible for their path to adulthood. Perfect changes are much harder at this point. Many factors are at play by this point in the child's development. If they are unhealthy and have an unhealthy surrounding then YOU are the one who will need to initiate the change. This change will be hard at this point but very worthwhile. Lead by example and do your best to recruit others to help you. Kids like fun so seek out fun experiences for your child and do your best to get them engaged in-group activities. Start substituting healthy options around the house, and make sure to listen to their input. Their involvement is crucial to their success. Success may not happen by the time they leave the house, but if you continue down the healthy road, there is a higher probability that they will come around.

Conclusion

We're surrounded with "reasons'" to not make the directional change to improve our health. There is little doubt that we know that being healthy is right thing to do but many of us are not doing it. We have to know our "whys" and then thoroughly address them. Face your insecurities by being honest with yourself. Find your stumbling block and address it. Do the soul searching! For the most part, we are not taking care of ourselves and we need to understand why we are not. This is a big deal. We need to address this issue. After our discovery, we need to ensure that we build an infrastructure around our reasons so they do not impede progress. Understand that YOU MATTER. There isn't anything that deserves being an issue. Overcoming our obstacles is empowering. A better you is worth seeking. Go ahead and have fun with your life. Be the turtle!

Our children are at the stage they're at. Evaluate them and determine the best course of action to ensure their approach to life is healthy based. Never dismiss that you as a parent are responsible for their pathway into adulthood. See to it that they believe that being healthy is critical to a fulfilling happy life. Include fun into your healthy approach to life. Listen to your kids, but be firm so that healthy always wins.

All of you are worth it!